JAPANESE
SOUL COOKING

¥900

ボイルホタテサーモン・マグロ丼 ¥500
(Boiled Scallop, Tuna & Salmon)

マグロ・しらす丼
(Tuna &Dried Whitebait)

・ゴ丼
amed Sea E
(Eel)

¥500

月見鉄火丼 ¥500
(Tuna & Soft-Boiled Egg)

イクラ・マグロ丼
(Tuna & Salmon Roe)

・アナゴ丼 ¥500
teamed Sea Eel)

サーモン・マグロ丼 ¥500
(Tuna & Salmon)

マグロ・明太

JAPANESE
SOUL COOKING

Tadashi Ono & Harris Salat

RAMEN, TONKATSU, TEMPURA, AND MORE
from THE STREETS and KITCHENS OF TOKYO
AND BEYOND

Photography by Todd Coleman

TEN SPEED PRESS
Berkeley

CONTENTS

For my wonderful wife, Manami, and daughters,
Sueh and Kiku—you're my inspiration.
—Tadashi

For Momoyo and our adorable little Gen,
already an adventurous nosher just his folks.
—Harris

ACKNOWLEDGMENTS

We'd like to thank our editor Melissa Moore, art director Toni Tajima, and the rest of the Ten Speed Press gang; our agent Angela Miller; our pal, travel buddy, and mad photo genius Todd Coleman; the good folks at the Japan National Tourism Organization, the Tokyo Visitors and Convention Bureau, and the Tokyo Metropolitan Government for their phenomenal support and assistance; the Japan Maritime Self-Defense Force for inviting us to eat curry on a warship; the captain and crew of the JMSDF Notojima; our ever-gracious JMSDF liaison Lt. Commander Takashi Nobukuni; curry (and every other kind of Japanese cooking) *shisho* Nobuko Torimitsu and her friends; Tokyo food blogger Heimin Kaneko and his friends; the journalist Keiko Tsuyama; Chef Kazuyuki Takekawa of Daiki ramen; the owners and staff of all the Tokyo restaurants we visited, chowed down at, and photographed; our stellar researcher, Tomoko Mori; *Saveur* editor Jim Oseland, and Hilary Merzbacher, Sarah Green, Judy Haubert, Nidhi Chaudhry, and Helen Yin in the *Saveur* kitchen who helped make our food shoot possible; and our amazing recipe testers around the world—you rock!

INTRODUCTION

Let's start with a groundbreaking moment back in 1872, when Emperor Meiji of Japan did something no other ruler of that country had done for a thousand years, namely, bite into a juicy hunk of meat in public. That simple act stunned his subjects—and forever changed the course of Japanese culture. It gave birth to a new kind of cooking in Japan, a new kind of hearty, rib-sticking *comfort* food cooking that's beloved there to this day. It's a world apart from traditional Japanese standards like miso soup, grilled fish, and pickled vegetables, and it's the amazing—and surprising—cooking that we celebrate in this book.

But how could a singular chomp shake up an entire country?

Nineteen years earlier, in 1853, American warships had suddenly appeared in the Japanese port of Yokohama. Until then, the country's leaders had sealed off Japan from the rest of the world for more than two hundred years, during which time Japanese couldn't leave on pain of death. But while Japan faced inward those two centuries, America and European nations exploded into the most powerful economic and military powers on earth. So when Yankee warships showed up, and then demanded Japan open their doors to trade—or else—the Japanese had little choice but to accept.

Soon more Westerners planted themselves in Japan. Their arrival triggered a profound upheaval in the country that led to the formation of a modern state under the emperor, who was determined to launch an industrial revolution and build a modern military just like in the West.

Foreigners arriving in Japan brought with them strange and new ingredients, dishes, and eating habits—many of these centered on consuming meat. Up to then, meat eating in Japan was taboo, actually banned by Buddhist edict for a millennium. During their period of isolation, Japanese relied primarily on fish, vegetables, tofu, and traditional seasonings like dashi, miso, and soy sauce. But the emperor and his minions credited meat and dairy eating for the strapping physiques of the Westerners, who towered over Japanese at the time. So they urged Japanese to consume meat and other Western foods. The emperor's very public meat encounter followed, and soon after that, in 1873, an official banquet was thrown in Japan for a visiting Italian royal, where, for the first time, this formal meal was prepared entirely of French cuisine.

These seminal events got the Western cuisine ball rolling, and before long, eating Western-style cuisine became a powerful symbol of modernity in Japan.

In the late nineteenth century, Western-style restaurants began to appear in Japan, like *Seiyo-ken* ("Western House"), which opened its doors in Tokyo in 1872. At the same time, the Japanese military began adopting Western-style foods. From these beginnings, ordinary Japanese began to learn of this new style of eating. Chefs, food companies, and cooks began to adapt these dishes to Japanese tastes, mixing and matching both Western and local ingredients, such as butter and soy sauce. Within a few decades, the mass media, especially women's magazines and radio shows, began featuring this cooking. What started as restaurant fare, like tonkatsu, or military chow, like curry, began to filter into homes across Japan. By the first half of the twentieth century, Chinese and Korean dishes like ebi chili, bulgogi, and chahan, also adapted to Japanese tastes, joined Western cooking in this culinary march. And in the years after World War II, Americans occupying Japan added their own unique food influences, including Japanese-style (*wafu*) pasta.

The embrace of foreign food evolved in Japan into a parallel cuisine, comfort food cooking that became as beloved as traditional Japanese fare. This modern style of eating picked up steam as Japan became increasingly urbanized, and we consider even stalwart dishes like soba, udon, and tempura to be a part of it.

What fascinates us, as you'll read in the pages that follow, are how so many of the dishes we describe began life as restaurant cooking, but then were quickly embraced by home cooks. And even today, these dishes are enjoyed both at neighborhood eateries and at the dining table. And that's key. Because, as you'll see in the pages that follow, these dishes are as delicious and amazing as they are simple and easy to whip up.

We organize our book by greatest hits, so soon you'll be swooning over ramen, gyoza, curry, tonkatsu, furai, okonomiyaki, *wafu* pasta, and all the other dishes we introduce here, just like Japanese everywhere. Packed with flavor, easy to cook, and totally irresistible, these recipes will have you at the first bite. Enjoy!

当店自慢の
基本のメニュー

No.1
850円 辛ごま
つけ麺

ごまの交わいた とろ
とろ
のつけダレ!!

No.2
しびれ系
味噌らーめん 花椒の香りと
880円 とうがらしの辛みを含め
こだわり せ少しびれるスープ
のスープ

魚系+動物系

豚骨、鶏ガラ
昆布、鯖節、宗田節
香味野菜、干ししいたけ
圧力なべ使用♡

土曜は
時まで
営業しております

1 RAMEN

RAMEN

In Japan, ramen is much more than a tasty bowl of noodles—it borders on an obsession. Forget that cheapo "cup ramen" you downed to fuel college all-nighters. What we're talking about is perfection in a bowl: a rich broth labored over for hours; fresh, springy wheat noodles; savory, mouthwatering seasonings; and toppings like slices of tender braised meat and creamy soft-boiled egg. But ramen isn't some high-concept cuisine, and that's the beauty of it. These noodles can be one of the most amazing things you've ever tasted, but this dish is about as down-home and down-to-earth as it gets. In Japan, the most famous ramen joints—in fact, the ones with endless lines and cult followings—are typically hole-in-the-wall operations with open kitchens and tight dining counters, run by cooks wearing T-shirts and towels wrapped around their heads like biker bandanas.

Let's back up and take a minute to dissect a bowl. So what exactly makes ramen, ramen? Four things are key. First, there's the soup (even in Japan, ramen soup is called by the English word "soup"), conjured from pork bones, chicken bones, kombu, and/or dried, shaved bonito, and cooked in huge vats for hours to tease out flavors (even several *days* for all-pork-bone soup). Second, there's the *tare*, a concentrated flavor essence of traditional Japanese seasonings like soy sauce and miso that define a particular style of ramen. Third, there are the wheat noodles, which, depending on the region (we'll get to that in a moment), can vary from straight to wavy, and from thin to thick. And finally, there are the toppings, which traditionally include *chashu*, delectable slices of braised pork (sometimes chicken); slow-cooked eggs, often steeped in a soy sauce marinade; thin-sliced scallion or Japanese *negi* onion; pickled bamboo shoots; and/or sheets of nori seaweed. Different regions also add their own special toppings.

Through some awesome-to-behold handiwork, experienced ramen cooks assemble these bowls by mixing soup and *tare* at the same time they're cooking and straining fresh noodles, then finishing the dish with the chosen toppings, a culinary two-step that's usually danced in under two minutes so that the ramen is served with soup piping hot and awesomely fragrant, and noodles perfectly toothsome, springy, and irresistible.

So now that you understand ramen basics, let's talk about the main styles of this dish. These noodles are an adaptation of Chinese soupy noodles in broth that first hit Japan in the late nineteenth century. (Originally, they were called *shina soba*, "Chinese noodles.") But it wasn't until the end of World War II that they became cultishly beloved, when repatriated Japanese soldiers brought home with them a love for noodles they had tasted overseas. Also, Americans who had occupied Japan supplied vast amounts of wheat flour to the war-torn country. As a result, many ex-soldiers set up ramen businesses to support themselves, often cooking from pushcarts. From there, ramen quickly evolved and acquired regional characteristics.

We count at least twenty distinct regional styles of ramen in Japan (although *ramen otaku*—the ramen obsessed—might quibble with this number and argue it's too low). Of these, three primary styles have emerged: Tokyo soy sauce ramen, Sapporo miso ramen, and Hakata tonkotsu ramen.

With Tokyo ramen, the soup is traditionally cooked from chicken bones, pork bones, and *wafu* ingredients (Japanese staples like dried, shaved bonito and kombu). The *tare*, the concentrated flavor essence, is based on soy sauce, and the noodles are wavy and thin. The clear, fragrant soup is sometimes topped with spinach, in addition to *chashu*, eggs, scallions, bamboo shoots, and nori.

Sapporo ramen hails from the capital of the northernmost main island of Hokkaido. In this snowy, rugged land, ramen joints cook a fatty, rich pork and chicken soup; make a *tare* from deep, savory miso; and use thick, wavy noodles produced with more alkaline and eggs to impart a shiny gloss and extra springiness (*tsuru-tsuru* is what they call this singular texture). All that fat, besides tasting amazing, also forms a layer on top that keeps the noodles and soup hot (especially in poorly heated hole-in-the-wall places). It's delicious and practical. Classic Sapporo toppings include ground pork, cabbage, bean sprouts, butter, and corn, of all things (Hokkaido is a dairy and corn-growing region).

Then there's Hakata ramen, which originated in Japan's deep south. This style uses pork bones (and sometimes heads and other parts) that are cooked over high heat for up to several days to tease out the essence of the marrow, resulting in a funky, milky white soup. Hakata ramen traditionally doesn't use any *tare*. The noodles are thin and straight and typically barely cooked (for just seconds). The toppings are usually limited to *chashu* and scallions, but Hataka ramen joints keep condiments like grated garlic, sesame seed, *beni shoga* (red pickled ginger), and sometimes pickled spicy mustard greens (*takana*) handy for customers to add themselves.

Okay, these are the broad strokes—just remember that even *within* each style, cooks endlessly tinker with them.

We know what you're thinking now: ramen seems cool, and deep—but how the heck (feel free to substitute with a stronger word) can you possibly cook this at home? (Pork bones for three days!) We're glad you asked. As you'll discover in the recipes that follow, we break down the soup, *chashu*, slow-cooked eggs, and recipes—for seven kinds of ramen—so that anyone can cook them. Believe us, it's totally doable. And we'll venture a bet that, before long, you'll be wrapping a towel around your head yourself and charging admission to your dining room for ramen night. (Admittedly, we might be getting carried away. But you'll see, you'll get into it.)

We base all our ramen recipes on Tadashi's adaptation of a master Tokyo-style soup recipe, which works great with other styles, too. (Except for Hakata ramen, the authentic version of which is basically impossible to cook at home.) And we include a number of regional and specialty ramens to try, all delicious. So pull out that head towel and go to town!

A Few Words about Ramen Noodles

In Japan, the type of noodle used in ramen is serious business. Thick or thin, straight or wavy, yellowish or not yellowish (the list goes on)—the noodle itself helps define a particular style of this dish. It would be sacrilege for, say, a Hakata joint to cook its local ramen with Sapporo-style thick, wavy noodles. But home cooks here, alas, don't have the luxury of choosing exactly the right kind of noodle. So what to do? Easy. Don't sweat it. Buy whatever ramen noodles you can find, and use them for any of the dishes that follow. You can usually buy fresh-frozen ramen noodles at Japanese and Asian markets, as well as dry varieties. Sometimes these noodles come with a soup mix. In this case, throw out the mix, and keep the noodles. Also, if there's a Chinatown near you, you can find fresh Cantonese egg noodles. These are great—go with the thin variety.

Anatomy of Ramen

scallions

soup

noodles

nori

pickled menma

spinach

pork shoulder

soy sauce eggs

RAMEN SOUP AND CHASHU Master Recipe

A round of applause goes to Tadashi for creating a home cook's version of ramen soup from scratch. As we mentioned earlier, this recipe is Tadashi's adaptation of Tokyo's prototypical clean, fragrant ramen soup. Note that we cook the pork shoulder for *chashu* along with the stock ingredients. *Chashu* is slow-braised meat that's simmered until tender. It's then sliced and laid on top of ramen noodles. The way we cook it, in the soup, is the way real ramen joints do—a one-two punch that adds richness and flavor to both the soup and the tender pork. You can prepare a batch of ramen soup ahead of time, and keep it in the freezer for up to one month. For the *chashu*, fresh pork belly or pork loin also works great.

MAKES 2 QUARTS

2 pounds chicken bones (bones and carcass)

½ ounce ginger, skin left on

2 cloves garlic, peeled

1 pound boneless pork shoulder (one piece, ask your butcher to tie it, if needed)

3 quarts water

1 scallion

½ small carrot (about 2 ounces)

Rinse the chicken bones well under cold running water. Crush the ginger by placing a kitchen knife over the ginger, and press down on the knife with your palm. Repeat for the garlic. Add all the ingredients to a large stockpot, and place on a burner over high heat. When the liquid boils, reduce the heat and simmer uncovered. Skim off any scum that accumulates on the surface and discard. Simmer for about 2 hours, until the soup reduces to 2 quarts. Remove the pork shoulder and set aside for *chashu*. (If you're not using it right away, store it in the refrigerator.) Strain the soup through a cheesecloth-lined colander or fine-mesh sieve, discarding the remaining ingredients.

All-Chicken Variation Substitute 1 pound of boneless chicken for the pork shoulder (we prefer dark meat, but white meat is fine, too). Use this chicken for *chashu* in the recipes that follow.

SOY SAUCE MARINADE

Master Recipe

Use this marinade for flavoring the soy sauce eggs and *chashu* in the recipes that follow. To make it, we combine Japanese seasonings brimming with umami together with fresh aromatics, bring them to a boil, then let the flavors mingle. Simple but potent, this marinade will infuse eggs and pork with complex, alluring flavors. Store it in the refrigerator for up to one month.

MAKES ABOUT 2 3/4 CUPS

1 cup water

1 cup soy sauce

1/2 cup sake

1/4 cup mirin

2 cloves garlic, peeled and crushed

2 scallions (about 2 ounces), trimmed and coarsely chopped

1 ounce ginger, skin on, crushed

2 pieces star anise (optional)

Add all the ingredients to a saucepan. Bring to a boil over high heat. Remove from the heat and allow to come to room temperature.

SOY SAUCE EGGS Master Recipe

Ajitama, we love you. A seasoned, soft-boiled egg sliced lengthwise, the yolk creamy and delicious, the whites impregnated with subtle soy sauce flavor, this is the egg that rests atop ramen noodles and broth, beckoning your chopsticks. In Japan, these eggs seem almost luminous, with the yolk varying in hue from sunflower yellow to the red of the setting sun. (All created naturally—the variety of eggs in Japan is awesome.) A few practical notes to keep in mind: First, use eggs right out of the refrigerator so the raw yolk is as cold as possible, which will prevent it from cooking through. Also, we ask you to punch a tiny hole in the eggshell before cooking. This helps loosen the egg white from the shell during cooking, making it easier to peel. Finally, you'll see we also ask you to spin the eggs while they cook. Why spin? The centrifugal force causes the yolks to set in the center of the egg, which looks more beautiful (and the centered yolk also helps with peeling).

MAKES 4 EGGS

4 eggs

2 cups soy sauce marinade (opposite)

Fill a saucepan with water and bring to a boil over high heat. When the water boils, reduce the heat to medium.

Use a pushpin or other stiff pin to gently open a small hole on the bottom of each egg (the rounded side is the bottom, rather than the pointy side). Be careful not to break the shell elsewhere.

Gently place the eggs in the boiling water. Cook for 5 to 7 minutes (5 minutes for a runny yolk, 7 minutes for a firmer, yet still soft, yolk). For the first 2 minutes of cooking, use a spoon or chopsticks to spin the eggs around in the saucepan.

When the eggs are ready, pour out the boiling water, and place the saucepan under cold, running water to cool the eggs. When the eggs are cool, peel them.

Pour the marinade into a bowl and add the peeled eggs. Marinate the eggs in the refrigerator for up to 12 hours. (The longer they marinate, the more pronounced the soy sauce flavor, as you desire.) The eggs will keep in the refrigerator for 1 week.

Ramen

SHOYU RAMEN

Time to whip up some amazing ramen! As we mentioned earlier, these noodles are the original Tokyo style, whose *tare*, the concentrated flavor essence, is based on *shoyu* (soy sauce). You'll be amazed by how good this ramen will turn out. A few things to keep in mind: Make sure you prepare the master recipes for the soup, *chashu*, marinade, and soy sauce eggs well ahead of time, so everything is ready before you start this recipe (you can prepare the master recipes a day or two in advance). Also, in the recipe that follows, *chashu* must marinate for about 20 minutes, so add that to your timing calculus, too. There's a specific order to assembling this ramen: add the *tare* first, then pour in the soup, then drop in the noodles, then layer on the toppings. And don't forget—the soup has to be hot, hot, hot. Finally, the soy sauce *tare* will keep for a month in the refrigerator, so make this ramen early and often.

SERVES 4

soy sauce tare

1 cup soy sauce

¼ cup sake

1 tablespoon mirin

½ ounce ginger, peel on and crushed

1 scallion, trimmed and coarsely chopped

1 clove garlic, peeled and crushed

1 bunch spinach (about 1 pound), trimmed and cleaned

chasu

2⅔ cups soy sauce marinade (page 10)

1 pound cooked pork shoulder (page 9), cooled to room temperature

4 packages (about 6 ounces each) fresh-frozen ramen noodles

2 quarts ramen soup (page 9), hot

4 soy sauce eggs (page 11), each cut in half

4 ounces menma (pickled bamboo)

4 sheets nori (2 inches by 2 inches)

1 scallion, trimmed and coarsely chopped

Prepare the *tare* by adding the ingredients to a saucepan and placing over high heat. When the liquid comes to a boil, turn off the heat.

To prepare the spinach, fill a large saucepan with water and bring to a boil over high heat. Add the spinach and blanch for 1 minute. Transfer the spinach to a colander and shock under cold, running water. When the spinach has cooled, arrange spinach in a one row on a work surface, alternating the stem and leaf ends. Use your hands to squeeze the row of spinach over the sink to expel excess water. Cut into 4 portions and set aside.

To prepare the *chashu*, pour the soy sauce marinade into a bowl. Add the pork shoulder piece and marinate for 20 minutes at room temperature. Transfer the pork shoulder to a cutting board and slice into ⅛-inch slices. Divide the slices into 4 portions and set aside.

To prepare the ramen, fill a large stockpot with water and place over high heat. Ready 4 large bowls on a work surface. When the water boils, add the noodles. Stir the noodles for about 10 seconds, so they separate and cook evenly. Cook for about 2 minutes, until the noodles are cooked through and toothsome. While the noodles are cooking, pour into each bowl

continued >

1/4 cup of the *tare* and 2 cups of the hot ramen soup.

When the noodles are ready, drain them into a colander. Carefully divide the noodles among the 4 bowls, being careful not to splash the hot soup. For each bowl, assemble the ramen by arranging the

1 portion of *chashu*, 1 egg (both halves), 1 ounce of *menma*, 1 portion of spinach, and 1 sheet of nori over the noodles. (See the photo on page 12 for how to arrange.) Garnish with the scallions and serve piping hot.

How to Eat Ramen

Here's the first thing that strikes you at a serious ramen joint in Japan: the near total silence. You'd think the customers would be hanging out with friends, shooting the breeze while downing great noodles, and knocking back brewskies. But no. Cooks will shout out orders, but customers cut the chitchat and instead hunch over their ramen, slurping up noodles like the clock is ticking. And in fact, the clock *is* ticking, figuratively anyway. The golden rule of ramen is . . . shut up and eat. First, savor the soup while it's hot—and we mean hot. At a top ramen joint, the soup arrives almost boiling, the better to impart its mouthwatering fragrance. Then, slurp (loudly!) the noodles while they're still perfectly cooked and toothsome. Loud slurping is important because it (a) cools the noodles before they reach your lips, (b) sucks up additional delicious soup, and (c) signals to the ramen chef that you appreciate his or her hard labor! Only after you've sipped the soup and slurped some noodles do you tuck into the toppings, alternating bites between all the foods in your bowl. The entire experience shouldn't last more than ten minutes. And finally, you don't have to finish all the soup, which is usually strongly salted to wake up the palate and balance the blander noodles. But you must—always—slurp up every last bit of noodle.

MISO RAMEN

This is our version of Sapporo's hearty classic ramen, using our master recipes to pull it together. Just like in that snowy city, we add cabbage and bean sprouts to this dish. But if other common Sapporo toppings like corn or butter move you, don't hesitate to add them, too. Here, the *chashu* isn't marinated, so as not to overpower the miso-based soup. Grate the garlic instead of chopping or pressing it, the better to break down its cells and release all that glorious garlicky heat. And add *tobanjan* if you like your ramen hot. Fermented from fava beans and chiles, this fiery condiment will bestow a glorious kick. You can find mung bean sprouts at Asian markets. The miso *tare* will keep in the refrigerator for up to a month.

miso tare

¼ cup sake

3 tablespoons mirin

2 cloves garlic, grated

1 teaspoon grated ginger

½ cup Sendai miso (or other aged red miso)

1 teaspoon tobanjan (optional; see page 236)

2 tablespoons sesame oil

¾ pound ground pork

4 teaspoons finely chopped scallion, white parts only

8 ounces cabbage, cored and coarsely chopped

2 quarts ramen soup (page 9), hot

8 ounces mung bean sprouts (moyashi)

4 packages (about 6 ounces each) fresh-frozen ramen noodles

1 pound cooked pork shoulder (page 9), cut into ⅛-inch slices and divided into 4 portions

4 soy sauce eggs (page 11), each cut in half

¼ cup chopped scallion

1 tablespoon ground sesame

Prepare the *tare* by adding the sake, mirin, garlic, and ginger to a saucepan. Bring to a boil over medium heat. Remove from the heat. Add the miso and *tobanjan*. Whisk until the miso is well combined with the other ingredients.

To prepare the pork, heat the sesame oil in a large saucepan over medium heat. Add the ground pork and scallion and cook for about 30 seconds, stirring and breaking up the pork into small pieces. Add the cabbage and cook, stirring frequently, for 1 minute more. Add the ramen soup. Cook for 2 minutes. Add the miso *tare*. When the soup comes to a boil, reduce the heat to low and cook for 1 minute. Turn off the heat.

Fill a large saucepan with water and bring to boil over high heat. Add the bean sprouts to the boiling water and blanch for 1 minute. Transfer to a colander and drain.

To prepare the ramen, fill a large stockpot with water and place over high heat. Ready 4 large bowls on a work surface. When the water boils, add the noodles. Stir the noodles for about 10 seconds, so they separate and cook evenly. Cook for about 2 minutes, until the noodles are cooked through and toothsome.

continued >

Ramen

When the noodles are ready, drain them into a colander. Divide the noodles among the 4 bowls. Pour one-fourth of the miso soup base into each bowl, making sure the pork, cabbage, and sprouts are divided evenly. For each bowl, assemble the ramen by arranging the 1 portion of pork shoulder, 1 egg (both halves), and 1 portion of bean sprouts over the noodles. Garnish with the scallions and sesame, and serve piping hot.

SHIO RAMEN

SERVES 4

Shio is the Japanese word for "salt," and it describes a style of ramen that originated in the city of Hakodate, which, like Sapporo, is located in the rugged confines of the snowy Japanese island of Hokkaido. But unlike Sapporo's thick, hearty miso soup, the Hakodate version is flavored only with salt. What a difference a hundred miles makes (as the stork flies). We love this style, too (as you might have guessed, we love ALL styles of ramen). It's clean and light, and a delight to slurp down. Don't marinate the *chashu* for this ramen. Also, we like to use *arajio* for this recipe, which is an incredible, minerally Japanese sea salt still wet with ocean brine. You can find it in Japanese markets. Or use any good sea salt you have on hand. Finally, the *shio tare* will keep in the refrigerator for a month.

shio tare

2 tablespoons finely chopped ginger

1 tablespoon finely chopped garlic

2 tablespoons finely chopped scallion, white parts only

¼ cup toasted sesame oil

1 cup sake

¼ cup sea salt

4 ounces cabbage, cored and cut into bite-size pieces

8 ounces mung bean sprouts (moyashi)

4 packages (about 6 ounces each) fresh-frozen ramen noodles

2 quarts ramen soup (page 9), hot

1 pound cooked pork shoulder (page 9), cut into ⅛-inch slices and divided into 4 portions

4 soy sauce eggs (page 11), each cut in half

4 sheets nori (2 inches by 2 inches)

¼ cup chopped scallion

Prepare the *tare* by adding the ginger, garlic, scallion, and sesame oil to a small saucepan. Place over medium-low heat and simmer for 2 minutes. Carefully pour in the sake and add the salt. Turn the heat to high and bring to a boil. Boil for 1 minute. Turn off the heat.

To prepare the cabbage, fill a large saucepan with water and bring to a boil over high heat. Add the cabbage leaves and blanch for 5 minutes. Transfer the cabbage to a colander (keep the boiling water in the saucepan). Cool under cold, running water. Drain, and divide into 4 portions.

Add the bean sprouts to the boiling water and blanch for 1 minute. Transfer to a colander, drain, and divide into 4 portions. Set aside.

To prepare the ramen, fill a large stockpot with water and place over high heat. Ready 4 large bowls on a work surface. When the water boils, add the noodles. Stir the noodles for about 10 seconds, so they separate and cook evenly. Cook for about 2 minutes, until the noodles are cooked through and toothsome. While the noodles are cooking, pour into each bowl

3 tablespoons of *tare* and 2 cups of hot ramen soup.

When the noodles are ready, drain them into a colander. Carefully divide the noodles among the 4 bowls, being careful not to splash the hot soup. For each bowl, assemble the ramen by arranging the 1 portion of pork shoulder, 1 egg (both halves), 1 portion of cabbage, 1 portion of bean sprouts, and 1 sheet of nori over the noodles. Garnish with the scallion and serve piping hot.

Ramen

TAN TAN MEN

This style of ramen was inspired by super spicy Sichuanese-style dan dan noodles. While the Japanese version isn't nearly as hot, it still packs a pleasing punch. Tan tan men is also infused with wonderful sesame paste and aromatics like ginger and garlic, so a lot is going on here. Because of all these flavors, we use a simple *torigara*, a chicken-bones-and-water Japanese-style chicken stock (page 25), as the foundation for this dish. Also, keep in mind that this is a basic version of this dish and you can play around with it. Like it head-melting spicy? Add more *rayu* (page 35). Like it less soupy (like the original Chinese version)? Serve with less liquid. Any way you go, this is a great ramen dish.

1 tablespoon toasted sesame oil

2 tablespoons finely chopped scallion, white parts only

1 teaspoon finely chopped ginger

1 teaspoon finely chopped garlic

8 ounces ground pork

1 tablespoon tobanjan (see page 236)

6 cups torigara stock (page 25), or 6 cups water plus 2 tablespoons torigara base

2 tablespoons soy sauce

1 teaspoon sugar

5 tablespoons Japanese sesame paste

2 teaspoons salt

4 packages (about 6 ounces each) fresh-frozen ramen noodles

¼ cup thinly sliced scallion, white and green parts

Rayu (page 35, optional)

To prepare the broth, add the sesame oil, finely chopped scallion, ginger, and garlic to a large saucepan and heat over high heat. Cook, stirring constantly, for about 1 minute to release their aroma. Add the pork and *tobanjan* and cook, stirring constantly, for about 2 minutes, until the pork turns white. Break the pork apart as you stir. Add the *torigara* stock, soy sauce, sugar, sesame paste, and salt. Bring the liquid to a boil, then reduce the heat to a simmer. Cook for about 3 minutes, stirring occasionally, so the flavors can combine. Turn off the heat.

To prepare the ramen, fill a large stockpot with water and place over high heat. Ready 4 large bowls on a work surface. When the water boils, add the noodles.

Stir the noodles for about 10 seconds, so they separate and cook evenly. Cook for about 2 minutes, until the noodles are cooked through and toothsome. While the noodles are cooking, turn the heat on the broth to high.

When the noodles are ready, drain them into a colander. Divide the noodles among the 4 bowls. Pour one-fourth of the tan tan broth over each bowl of noodles. Garnish with the thinly sliced scallions and serve piping hot. Accent with the *rayu* to taste.

NAGASAKI CHAMPON

Nagasaki, located on the southwestern main island of Kyushu, is an old trading port that attracted Chinese students in the nineteenth century. Naturally, restaurants popped up to serve their home-style chow. In 1899, at one of these places, a Fujianese chef named Hejun Chin invented a dish based on his native Fujian-style noodles—a dish that evolved into today's Nagasaki champon, which soon became popular across the country. The word *champon* refers to something mixed, and indeed these noodles are a satisfying combination of seafood, pork, and vegetables, all served in a mouthwatering soup. In restaurants, slow-cooked pork bones (like with tonkotsu ramen, page 7) give this soup a milky appearance; we use actual milk to create this effect, plus to add body and flavor. Traditional champon noodles are thicker and wider than regular ramen noodles, but the ramen version is fine to use. If you like heat, add a dab of *tobanjan* (spicy fermented bean paste, see page 236) to spice things up.

SERVES 4

2 tablespoons sesame oil

4 ounces thinly sliced pork (available at Asian markets), cut into bite-size pieces

3 cloves garlic, peeled and thinly sliced

4 ounces squid, cleaned and sliced into rings

4 ounces scallops, cut into 1/2-inch-thick slices

4 ounces small shrimp (51/60 size), peeled

1 small carrot (about 3 ounces), peeled and sliced into 2-inch-long pieces

1/2 onion (about 8 ounces), peeled and cut into 1/4-inch-thick slices

4 ounces shiitake mushrooms, stems removed and sliced

4 ounces cabbage, cut into bite-size pieces

1/2 cup sake

2 quarts ramen soup (page 9), hot

1 tablespoon salt

1 tablespoon soy sauce

2 tablespoons mirin

2 cups milk

4 scallions, trimmed and sliced on an angle into 1-inch pieces

4 packages (about 6 ounces each) fresh-frozen ramen noodles

1 tablespoon ground sesame

To prepare the champon soup, heat the sesame oil in a saucepan over high heat. Add the pork and garlic and cook, stirring constantly, for 30 seconds. Add the squid, scallops, and shrimp, and cook, stirring constantly, for 30 seconds more. Add the carrot and onion, and cook and stir for 1 minute. Add the shiitake mushrooms and napa cabbage, cooking and stirring for 1 minute. Add the sake and cook for 30 seconds. Add the ramen soup, salt, soy sauce, and mirin. Cook for 2 minutes. Add the milk and scallions. Cook for 1 minute. Turn off the heat.

To prepare the ramen, fill a large stockpot with water and place over high heat. Ready 4 large bowls on a work surface. When the water boils, add the noodles. Stir the noodles for about 10 seconds, so they separate and cook evenly. Cook for about 2 minutes, until the noodles are cooked through and toothsome.

Drain the noodles into a colander and divide them among the 4 bowls. Pour one-fourth of the champon soup into each bowl, over the ramen. Make sure the pork, seafood, and vegetables are divided evenly. Garnish with ground sesame and serve piping hot.

HIYASHI CHUKKA

Okay, it's summer and it's hot as Hades outside. Ready for a steaming bowl of ramen? In case you aren't, here's a summertime ramen recipe where the noodles are served cold, sans soup. Perfect for any sweltering day. Literally, "cold Chinese noodles," Hiyashi Chukka is like a ramen salad, the cold toothsome noodles mixed with garnishes and drizzled with a tangy soy sauce–vinegar dressing. Super refreshing and delicious. Use "dry" cucumbers like Japanese, Persian, or hothouse. The egg in the dish, *kinshi tamago*, is a cooked as a paper-thin omelet that's sliced into thin strips. All you need now is a tall glass of iced tea and you're set.

½ **cup soy sauce**

½ **cup Japanese rice vinegar**

½ **cup torigara stock (page 25), or ½ cup water mixed with ½ teaspoon torigara base**

3 **tablespoons sugar**

½ **teaspoon salt**

2 **teaspoons toasted sesame oil**

4 **eggs**

4 **packages (about 6 ounces each) fresh-frozen ramen noodles**

4 **ounces thinly sliced ham, cut into strips**

2 **Japanese (or Persian) cucumbers (about 8 ounces), julienned**

1 **tomato (about 10 ounces), sliced**

4 **scallions, trimmed and sliced on an angle**

4 **teaspoons toasted sesame seed**

Karashi mustard (see page 234)

To prepare the dressing, ready an ice bath. Add the soy sauce, vinegar, torigara stock, sugar, salt, and 1 teaspoon of the sesame oil to a saucepan, and bring to a boil over medium heat. Place the saucepan in the ice bath and allow it to cool.

To prepare one thin omelet at a time, beat an egg well. Heat ¼ teaspoon of the sesame oil in a small skillet over medium heat. Add the egg and move it around to spread the egg over the entire skillet so it resembles a thin crepe. Cook for 30 seconds and carefully flip the egg. Cook for 15 seconds and transfer the omelet to a plate. Repeat with the remaining 3 eggs, stacking completed omelets on top of one another.

When all the omelets are prepared, roll up the stack of omelets and cut them into thin strips.

To prepare the ramen, fill a large stockpot with water and place over high heat. Ready 4 large bowls on a work surface. When the water boils, add the noodles. Stir the noodles for about 10 seconds, so they separate and cook evenly. Cook for about 2 minutes, until the noodles are cooked through and toothsome. When the noodles are ready, transfer them to a strainer and cool under cold running water. Set aside.

Divide the cold ramen noodles among 4 bowls. Top each bowl with one-fourth of the ham, cucumbers, tomato, scallions, and egg, arranging each ingredient in a separate, neat bunch. Pour one-fourth of the dressing over the ingredients in each bowl. Garnish with sesame seed and a dab of *karashi* mustard on the side of each bowl. Mix the ingredients together to eat.

SHRIMP WONTON MEN

Shrimp wontons are a Chinese import that are also a big favorite in Japan. Serving these tender, aromatic dumplings over noodles is a classic way to enjoy them in both cultures. Look for wonton skins, which are square shaped and thinner than gyoza skins. To make the dumplings, simply fold the skins into a triangular-shaped pocket.

SERVES 4

8 ounces small shrimp, shelled, cleaned, deveined, and finely chopped

2 tablespoons finely chopped scallion, white parts only

1 teaspoon finely chopped ginger

1 teaspoon sake

1 teaspoon plus 3 tablespoons soy sauce

1 teaspoon sesame oil

1 tablespoon katakuriko (potato starch), plus more for dusting

1/4 teaspoon plus pinch freshly ground black pepper

Pinch plus 1 teaspoon salt

About 20 wonton skins (2 inches by 2 inches)

1 tablespoon katakuriko (potato starch) mixed with 3 tablespoons warm water

6 cups torigara stock (page 25), or 6 cups water mixed with 2 tablespoons torigara base

2 packages (about 6 ounces each) fresh-frozen ramen noodles

1/4 cup finely sliced scallion, white and green parts

To prepare the wonton filling, add the shrimp, finely chopped scallion, ginger, sake, 1 teaspoon of the soy sauce, sesame oil, *katakuriko*, 1/4 teaspoon of the ground pepper, and pinch of the salt to a bowl. Use your hands to mix the ingredients together for at least 2 minutes. Press the ingredients with your hands, and squeeze them through your fingers; you want the shrimp mixture to become well blended and slightly sticky so it holds together while cooking.

To make the wontons, prepare a tray by lightly dusting with *katakuriko*. Place a wonton skin in the palm of one hand with the floured side down. (The skins are sold with one side floured.) Dip a finger in the katakuriko mixed with warm water and wet the entire edge of the skin. This water-starch mixture is the "glue" that will hold the skin closed. Add about 1/2 to 3/4 table-spoon of the shrimp filling to the center of the skin. Fold one corner of the skin over the other to form a triangular pocket. Pinch the skin together to seal it, and the wonton is done. Place the completed wonton on the tray, folded side up. Repeat until you've used up all the filling.

To prepare the soup, add the torigara stock, remaining 3 tablespoons soy sauce, remaining pinch pepper, and remaining 1 teaspoon salt to a large pot and bring to a boil over high heat. Reduce the heat to a simmer and add the wontons. Cook for

continued >

Ramen

about 2 minutes, until the wontons float to the surface. Reduce the heat to low.

To prepare the ramen, fill a large stockpot with water and place over high heat. Ready 4 large bowls on a work surface. When the water boils, add the noodles. Stir the noodles for about 10 seconds, so they separate and cook evenly. Cook for

about 2 minutes, until the noodles are cooked through and toothsome.

When the noodles are ready, drain them into a colander. Divide the noodles among the 4 bowls. Pour one-fourth of the soup over each bowl of noodles. Divide the wontons among the 4 bowls and garnish with the sliced scallions. Serve piping hot.

Torigara Stock

Torigara is Japanese-style chicken stock. It differs from the Western version in that it's made with bones and water to create a pure chicken essence; no roots (carrots, parsnips, etc.) or herbs (bay leaf, parsley, etc.) are added.

You can make torigara from scratch or use a premade base, which is sold as weiha in Japanese markets. To prepare premade torigara, mix 1 teaspoon base per 1 cup of water, then use as indicated in our recipes.

Finally, if you can't find the Japanese torigara base weiha, don't worry—just substitute with low-sodium or unsalted store-bought packages of all-natural chicken stock, which you can find in any supermarket.

MAKES 8 CUPS

1 pound chicken bones (wings and carcass okay too)

12 cups water, plus more for boiling

Place the chicken bones in a large pot and fill with enough water to cover, then bring to a boil over high heat. Strain the bones, discard the water, and rinse the bones under cold, running water to remove any scum. Return the bones to the pot, add the 12 cups of water, and bring to a boil again over high heat. Decrease the heat to medium and simmer until the stock reduces to approximately 8 cups, about 30 minutes. Remove any scum that appears on the surface as the stock is cooking. When it's ready, strain the liquid and discard the bones. Use now or store in the freezer, tightly covered, for up to 2 months.

2 GYOZA

GYOZA

Can two grown men swoon over a dumpling? Yes—if it's gyoza.

Japan's signature dumpling, gyoza is an import from China (like with ramen, the name derives from a Chinese word for dumplings). While there's mention of Chinese dumplings in an eighteenth-century Japanese cookbook, these pot stickers didn't take off until after World War II, when returning Japanese soldiers brought home a hankering for them, a hankering we can totally understand.

Gyoza are crescent-shaped dumplings, the classic version of which are filled with ground pork, cabbage, garlic, and garlic chives, and typically cooked *gyoza yaki*, a nifty frying-and-steaming technique that toasts the skin beautifully crispy on one side, while steaming it tender on the other side. Gyoza are usually dipped into a sauce of soy sauce, rice vinegar, and *rayu*, or flavored chili oil (check out our amazing homemade version, page 35). The dumplings come out crispy, juicy, aromatic, flavorful, heavenly, and irresistible all at once, with a pleasing tang and bite from the dipping sauce. Yep, enough to make us swoon.

The two main differences from their Chinese cousins (*jiaozi*) are the filling and the skin. Japanese use a lot more garlic, a throwback to the days after the war when gyoza were often made with strong-flavored mutton, which the garlic mollified. Also, Japanese dumpling skins are typically thinner than in China, and turn almost translucent on the steaming side. But the shape remains the same in both cultures—the crescent is a symbol of money, good luck, and fertility in China, and we guess Japanese didn't want to mess with success.

To many Japanese (and non-Japanese, such as Harris), "ramen, gyoza, beer" is the rallying call for a great meal, and we venture to say that in most ramen joints in Japan, you'll find gyoza on the menu (beer is a given). There are also gyoza specialty places, too, typically listing just three items on the menu, "gyoza, pickles, beer" (beer, always beer). Even entire cities weigh in when it comes to gyoza: in Osaka, bite-size versions rule, while a place called Utsunomia is so nuts about these dumplings that more than two hundred specialty gyoza shops are packed into that little city.

But gyoza isn't just the province of restaurants. *Au contraire, mon ami!* These dumplings do yeoman's work in home kitchens all across Japan. Once you get the handle on folding them (which we'll help you with, see page 32), they're a snap to make and freeze for later (see page 37). And besides the frying-and-steaming approach, you can poach gyoza in soup, steam them, or deep-fry them. You can also make these phenomenal dumplings with different ingredients, like chicken, shrimp, veggies, or even duck. And instead of the classic three-ingredient sauce, you can dip gyoza into oyster sauce or an amazing miso sauce (page 34).

CLASSIC PORK GYOZA Master Recipe

Here now, the Way of the Gyoza. Refer to our series of photographs, "How to Fold and Cook Gyoza" (page 32), as you go through this recipe. Once you fold a few thousand gyoza, you'll get the hang of the technique—we're kidding. Folding gyoza is pretty easy and you'll understand it quickly, but remember, it doesn't have to be perfect. Even if you just pinch the gyoza skins together and dispense with folding the skins like we do in the photos, your dumplings will turn out heavenly. Keep in mind a few things: Chop everything with a knife and do not use a food processor, which will turn the ingredients into mush, not the texture you want. You can use green, savoy, or napa cabbage (green is the default choice). Buy Japanese gyoza skins at Japanese markets; they are round in shape and thinner than their Chinese counterparts (and usually sold frozen; defrost on the counter to room temperature to use). When you cook them, the gyoza might stick together, and that's totally fine. But you can avoid this by separating the dumplings by about 1/8 inch when laying them in the pan. What you're looking for in the finished product is beautiful crispy brown bottoms and tenderly steamed tops. See our photos and you'll know what we mean. Finally, besides the classic dipping sauce we explain in the recipe, these gyoza are also amazing with our miso dipping sauce (page 34). And if you can't decide between the sauces—just make both and dip away!

MAKES ABOUT 50 GYOZA

3 cups trimmed and finely chopped green cabbage (about 8 ounces)

1/2 teaspoon salt

1 1/2 cups nira (Japanese green garlic chives), bottom 2 inches trimmed to remove the hard stem, and finely chopped (about 1/3 pound)

1 tablespoon finely chopped garlic (about 2 cloves)

1 tablespoon finely chopped ginger (about 1 ounce ginger, peeled)

2/3 pound ground pork

2 teaspoons soy sauce

4 tablespoons toasted sesame oil

1/2 teaspoon ground black pepper

1/2 teaspoon salt

2 teaspoons sugar

2 tablespoons katakuriko (potato starch), plus extra for dusting

50 round gyoza skins, 3 to 4 inches in diameter

1 tablespoon katakuriko (potato starch) mixed with 3 tablespoons warm water

Soy sauce

Japanese rice vinegar

Rayu (page 35)

2/3 cup water

To prepare the filling, add the cabbage and salt to a large bowl and thoroughly mix together. Let the cabbage sit at room temperature for 15 minutes. When it's ready, transfer the cabbage to a clean kitchen towel or large cheesecloth. Roll up the cloth and wring out the liquid in the cabbage, like you're wringing dry a wet towel.

This is a key step so the gyoza doesn't become watery. Wring out as much liquid from the cabbage as possible. Do this in batches if it's easier.

Add the wrung-out cabbage, *nira*, garlic, ginger, pork, soy sauce, 2 tablespoons of the sesame oil, black pepper, salt, sugar,

continued >

Gyoza

and *katakuriko* to a large bowl. Use your hands to mix the ingredients together for about 2 minutes. Mash and mush the mixture together, squeezing it through your fingers, so it turns into a sticky filling that will hold together when you spoon it into a dumpling skin.

To make the dumplings, prepare a tray by lightly dusting it with *katakuriko*. Place a gyoza skin in the palm of one hand with the floured side down. (The skins are sold with one side floured.) Dip a finger in the *katakuriko* mixed with warm water and wet the entire edge of the skin. This water-starch mixture is the "glue" that will hold the skin closed. Add about 1 tablespoon of the filling to the center of the skin. Use the index fingers and thumbs of both hands to fold the skin and pinch it together. See "How to Fold and Cook Gyoza" (page 32) for step-by-step instructions with photographs. Place the completed gyoza on the tray, fold side up. Repeat until you've used up all the filling.

To prepare the dipping sauce, combine the soy sauce, vinegar, and *rayu*. A classic proportion is 4 parts soy sauce to 2 parts vinegar to 1 part *rayu*. Adjust to your own taste. Pour the dipping sauce into individual small bowls and set aside.

To cook the gyoza, preheat a nonstick pan or cast-iron skillet over high heat for about 5 minutes. (We like to use a 12-inch-diameter skillet with a cover to prepare gyoza.) When the skillet is hot, add 1 table-spoon of the sesame oil, making sure the entire surface is coated (you can use a wadded-up paper towel to carefully spread the oil). Begin adding the gyoza, one at a time, in neat rows, with the seam side up. A 12-inch skillet will hold about 20 gyoza. Once all the gyoza are added, fry them for about 10 seconds. Now quickly pour in the water over the gyoza and cover the skillet tightly. Cook over high heat for about 4 minutes. Uncover the skillet; there should be little or no water remaining. Cook for 1 minute more. Drizzle the remaining 1 tablespoon sesame oil over the gyoza and cook for an additional 1 minute, for about 6 minutes total cooking time. The gyoza should look glossy with the skins cooked through. Turn off the heat and use a thin fish spatula to transfer the gyoza to a serving plate, this time with the seam side down (you want to show off the beautifully crispy, browned bottoms of the dumplings). Serve the dumplings steaming hot, with the dipping sauce on the side. Dip in the sauce to eat.

Variation You can substitute the salt and soy sauce in the gyoza filling with 2 table-spoons of red miso, for a savory twist.

How to Make Gyoza *Hane*

If you can't get enough of those crispy gyoza bottoms, you're in need of some serious *hane* action. *Hane* literally means "wings." When talking gyoza, *hane* is a crispy, papery crust that you can make to attach to the dumplings (hence the wings analogy). They're a nifty little bonus that gyoza aficionados just love. Making *hane* is easy: Mix about 1½ teaspoons flour into the ⅔ cup water you use to steam the dumplings, and follow the instructions in the gyoza recipes. The mixture will form a crust on the pan that sticks to the gyoza (as pictured opposite). Also, if you want gyoza with *hane*, we suggest you use a nonstick skillet to cook your gyoza, which will help you easily remove the dumplings and their wings when they're ready.

How to Fold and Cook Gyoza

Wet the edges of the gyoza skin

Spoon the filling into the center of the skin

Fold the skin so the edges touch

Pinch and fold the skin 5 or 6 times
with your thumb and index finger

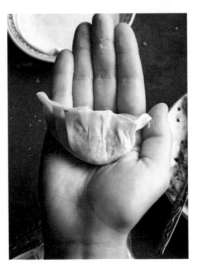

A folded gyoza

HOW TO COOK GYOZA, opposite:

1 Heat the skillet then add oil

2 Wipe off the excess oil

3 Lay gyoza in the pan

4 Fill the pan with gyoza and
fry for 10 seconds

5 Pour in water

6 Cover and steam for 4 minutes

7 Uncover and continue to cook until
all of the water evaporates

8 Drizzle in the remaining sesame oil

9 Remove the gyoza with
a fish spatula and serve

33

MISO DIPPING SAUCE Master Recipe

Use this delicious miso dipping sauce for any and all gyoza, but especially for our vegetarian and soup gyoza recipes. The sauce will keep in the refrigerator, tightly covered, for two weeks.

MAKES ABOUT 1/2 CUP

¼ cup Sendai miso (see page 235)

¼ cup torigara stock (page 25)

1 teaspoon toasted sesame oil

1 teaspoon finely chopped garlic

1 teaspoon finely chopped ginger

1 tablespoon finely chopped scallion, white parts only

1 tablespoon sugar

1 teaspoon tobanjan (see page 236)

¼ cup sake

1 tablespoon mirin

1 teaspoon vinegar

Whisk together the miso and *torigara* stock in a bowl. Set aside.

Heat the sesame oil in a skillet over medium heat. Add the garlic, ginger, and scallion, and cook, stirring constantly, for about 1 minute, to soften them. Add the sugar, *tobanjan*, sake, and mirin and bring to a boil. Add the miso-*torigara* mixture and cook, stirring constantly, for 1 minute, until the ingredients are combined. Add the vinegar and stir to combine. Cook for 15 seconds more, then turn off the heat. Allow the sauce to come to room temperature, and serve.

Japanese Beer

Sake, Japan's "national drink," might get all the glory, but beer is far and away the most popular alcoholic beverage in the country. First brewed in Japan at a beer hall for Dutch sailors in the seventeenth century, it really took off in the country a couple of hundred years later with the establishment of large breweries. Today there are hundreds of microbrewers crafting all types of beer, but the major brewers are the ones who set the quintessential style of Japanese beer. And that style can be summed up in one word—dry. Beers like Asahi Super Dry, Kirin Ichiban, and Sapporo are all crisp, light, bone-dry lagers that are the perfect thirst-quenching complement to Japanese cooking and flavors. Quaffing one of these brews from a frozen mug when going to town on gyoza or ramen is pure pleasure.

HOMEMADE RAYU

Master Recipe

Rayu is the flavored chili oil that spikes classic gyoza dipping sauce. You can certainly buy ho-hum bottled versions at Japanese markets, but they can't possibly compare to making this terrific homemade version brimming with fresh aromatics and glorious heat. Plus, you can add other aromatics and spices to create a personalized and an even more complex oil (see Variations, below). Store your bespoke *rayu* at room temperature, tightly sealed. It will keep for about 2 months.

MAKES ABOUT 1/2 CUP

1 tablespoon finely chopped ginger

1 tablespoon finely chopped garlic

1 tablespoon finely chopped scallion, white parts only

1/2 cup toasted sesame oil

1 tablespoon ichimi togarashi (see page 235) or ground Chinese red pepper

1 tablespoon coarse Chinese red pepper flakes

Add the ginger, garlic, scallion, and 1/4 cup of the sesame oil to a small saucepan. Place the saucepan over low heat and bring to a boil. Gently simmer for about 3 minutes over low heat, or until the ingredients turn golden. Gently swirl the pot while cooking to prevent the ingredients from burning. Pour the oil into a mixing bowl. Add the *ichimi togarashi* and coarse red pepper flakes, and mix to combine. Allow the oil to come to room temperature, and then add the remaining 1/4 cup toasted sesame oil. Transfer the rayu to a glass jar. To use, spoon the red rayu oil from the surface (so the chopped ingredients remain resting on the bottom). You can also strain the rayu through a fine sieve to remove the chopped ingredients from the oil, before pouring it into a storage jar.

Variations You can add 1 tablespoon of star anise, cinnamon, dried baby shrimp (called *okiami* or *hoshi ebi* in Japanese), Sichuan peppercorn, whole black pepper, and/or other aromatic spices to the *rayu* to create an even more complex flavor. Add these accents individually or in combination, but no more than two accents per recipe. (Otherwise, the flavor will become too muddled.)

SHRIMP SHISO GYOZA

Here's a delicious variation on classic gyoza with shrimp instead of pork. Shiso is an aromatic and flavorful fresh Japanese herb that adds a lovely punch to these dumplings. You can find shiso leaves (sometimes also called *ohba*) at Japanese markets.

MAKES ABOUT 50 GYOZA

3 cups trimmed and finely chopped napa cabbage (about 8 ounces)

1½ teaspoons salt

⅔ pound small shrimp, peeled, deveined, and finely chopped by hand

3 or 4 shiitake mushrooms (about 3 ounces), stemmed and finely chopped

10 shiso leaves, stems removed and finely chopped

3 tablespoons finely chopped scallion, white parts only (about 6 trimmed and washed scallions)

1 tablespoon finely chopped ginger

3 tablespoons dried baby shrimp

2 tablespoons katakuriko (potato starch)

4 tablespoons toasted sesame oil

50 round gyoza skins, 3 to 4 inches in diameter

1 tablespoon katakuriko (potato starch) mixed with 3 tablespoons warm water

Soy sauce

Japanese rice vinegar

Rayu (page 35)

⅔ cup water

To prepare the filling, add the cabbage and ½ teaspoon of the salt to a large bowl and thoroughly mix together. Let the cabbage sit at room temperature for 15 minutes. When it's ready, the cabbage will soften and appear translucent. Transfer the cabbage to a clean kitchen towel or large cheesecloth. Roll up the cloth and wring out the liquid in the cabbage, like you're wringing dry a wet towel. This is a key step so the gyoza doesn't become watery. Wring out as much liquid from the cabbage as possible. Do this in batches if it's easier.

Add the wrung-out cabbage, shrimp, shiitake, shiso, scallion, ginger, baby shrimp, *katakuriko*, 2 tablespoons of the toasted sesame oil, and remaining 1 teaspoon salt to a large bowl. Use your hands to mix the ingredients together for about 5 minutes. Mash and mush the mixture together, squeezing it through your fingers, so it turns into a sticky filling that will hold together when you spoon it into a dumpling skin.

To make the dumplings, prepare a tray by lightly dusting it with *katakuriko*. Place a gyoza skin in the palm of one hand with the floured side down. Dip a finger in the *katakuriko* mixed with warm water and wet the entire edge of the skin. This water-starch mixture is the "glue" that will hold the skin closed. Add about 1 tablespoon of the filling to the center of the skin. Use the index fingers and thumbs of both hands to fold the skin and pinch it together. See "How to Fold and Cook Gyoza" (page 32) for step-by-step instructions with photographs. Place completed gyoza on the tray, fold side up. Repeat until you've used up all the filling.

Prepare the dipping sauce by combining the soy sauce, vinegar, and *rayu*. A classic proportion is 4 parts soy sauce to 2 parts vinegar to 1 part *rayu*. Adjust to your own taste. Pour the dipping sauce into individual small plates and set aside.

To cook the gyoza, preheat a nonstick pan or cast-iron skillet over high heat for about 5 minutes. (We like to use a 12-inch-diameter skillet with a cover to prepare gyoza.) When the skillet is hot, add 1 tablespoon of the sesame oil, making sure the entire surface is coated (you can use a wadded-up paper towel to carefully spread the oil). Begin adding the gyoza, one at a time, in neat rows, with the seam side up. A 12-inch skillet will hold about 20 gyoza. Once all the gyoza are added, fry them for about 10 seconds. Now quickly pour in the water over the gyoza and cover the skillet tightly. Cook over high heat for about 4 minutes. Uncover the skillet; there should be little or no water remaining. Cook for 1 minute more. Drizzle the remaining 1 tablespoon sesame oil over the gyoza and cook for an additional 1 minute, for about 6 minutes total cooking time. The gyoza should look glossy with the skins cooked through. Turn off the heat and use a thin fish spatula to transfer the gyoza to a serving plate, this time with the seam side down (you want to show off the beautifully crispy, browned bottoms of the dumplings). Serve the dumplings steaming hot, with the dipping sauce on the side. Dip in the sauce to eat.

How to Freeze Gyoza

You might want to make a monster batch of gyoza (double or triple the recipe) and freeze the extra dumplings in nice rows that you can fit in your skillet, so you can easily transfer them to said skillet to cook. These rows are important, because to cook frozen gyoza you *don't* have to defrost. So you can always have a quick, amazing gyoza meal ready to go in your freezer. Just follow the cooking instructions on page 33, laying the frozen rows of dumplings directly into your skillet. But increase the cooking time to 8 minutes when the skillet is covered (instead of 4 minutes), for a total cooking time of about 10 minutes.

Gyoza

SOUP GYOZA WITH CHICKEN

So far we've made gyoza following the classic fry-and-steam *gyoza yaki* technique. Here we change things up and poach the dumplings in a soup. Tender, delicious, warming, and utterly satisfying, these poached gyoza are the perfect antidote to any blustery day. You eat these chicken gyoza by fishing them out of the soup and dipping into the dipping sauce, while sipping the soup on the side.

SERVES 4 (MAKES ABOUT 32 DUMPLINGS)

2 cups trimmed and finely chopped green cabbage (about 5 ounces)

2 ½ teaspoons salt

1 bunch scallions (about 5 scallions, or 4 ounces), trimmed and thinly sliced, plus 2 scallions (about 2 ounces), trimmed and green and white parts thinly sliced on an angle

1 teaspoon finely chopped garlic

1 teaspoon finely chopped ginger

1 tablespoon toasted sesame oil

8 ounces ground chicken

1 teaspoon sugar

1 tablespoon katakuriko (potato starch), plus extra for dusting

32 round gyoza skins, about 3 ½ inches in diameter

1 tablespoon katakuriko (potato starch) mixed with 3 tablespoons warm water

6 cups torigara stock (page 25), or 6 cups water with 1 ½ tablespoons torigara base

4 napa cabbage leaves (about 4 ounces), trimmed and sliced into bite-size pieces

Pinch pepper

½ cup miso dipping sauce (page 34), divided among 4 small bowls

---

To prepare the filling, add the chopped cabbage and 1 teaspoon of the salt to a large bowl and thoroughly mix together. Let the cabbage sit at room temperature for 15 minutes. Transfer the cabbage to a clean kitchen towel or large cheesecloth. Roll up the cloth and wring out the liquid in the cabbage, like you're wringing dry a wet towel. This is a key step so the gyoza doesn't become watery. Wring out as much liquid from the cabbage as possible. Do this in batches if it's easier. Set the cabbage aside.

Place the sliced scallions on a clean kitchen towel or large cheesecloth. Roll up the cloth and wring out the scallions like

you're wringing dry a wet towel. This time, don't wring as hard as with the cabbage; you want to gently wring just enough to expel the scallion's sliminess.

Add the cabbage, scallions, garlic, ginger, sesame oil, ground chicken, sugar, *katakuriko*, and ½ teaspoon of the salt to a large bowl. Use your hands to mix the ingredients together for about 3 minutes. Mash and mush the mixture together, squeezing it through your fingers, so it turns into a sticky filling that will hold together when you spoon it into a dumpling skin.

continued >

Gyoza

To make the dumplings, prepare a tray by lightly dusting it with *katakuriko*. Place a gyoza skin in the palm of one hand with the floured side down. Dip a finger in the potato starch mixed with warm water and wet the entire edge of the skin. This water-starch mixture is the "glue" that will hold the skin closed. Add about 3/4 tablespoon of the filling to the center of the skin. Use the index fingers and thumbs of both hands to fold the skin and pinch it together simply, like you're making a ravioli (for these gyoza, you don't have to use the pinch and fold technique like

for Classic Pork Gyoza). Place completed gyoza on the tray, fold side up. Repeat until you've used up all the filling.

To make the soup, add the *torigara* stock, napa cabbage, pepper, and the remaining 1 teaspoon salt to a large saucepan, and bring to a boil over medium heat. Add all the gyoza and cook, mixing occasionally, for about 3 minutes, until the gyoza are cooked through. Add the angle-sliced scallions, mix into the liquid, and turn off the heat. Serve immediately. Dip the gyoza in the miso sauce to eat.

VEGETARIAN GYOZA

Vegetarians, we humbly beseech you to share these singular gyoza with the omnivores in your life, too. In this recipe, Tadashi lavishes so many layers of flavors and textures— shiitake, garlic, ginger, miso, even pine nuts, and more—that anyone who loves gyoza will love these dumplings, guaranteed. Dip them in miso dipping sauce (page 34) for the perfect savory complement.

MAKES ABOUT 32 GYOZA

2 bunches spinach (about 2 pounds), stems trimmed

1 pound firm tofu (1 standard package)

4 ounces shiitake mushrooms (about 8 mushrooms), stems removed and chopped

1 teaspoon finely chopped garlic

1 teaspoon finely chopped ginger

1/4 cup finely chopped scallion, green and white parts

2 tablespoons Sendai miso or other red miso (see page 234)

2 tablespoons pine nuts, toasted and chopped

3 tablespoons toasted sesame oil

1 tablespoon sugar

1 tablespoon katakuriko (potato starch), plus extra for dusting

32 round gyoza skins, 3 to 4 inches in diameter

1 tablespoon katakuriko (potato starch) mixed with 3 tablespoons warm water

2/3 cup water

1/2 cup miso dipping sauce (page 34), divided among 4 small bowls

To prepare the spinach, place a large pot of water over high heat and bring to a boil. Add the spinach and blanch for 30 seconds, until the leaves turn bright green. Transfer the spinach to a colander and rinse under cold, running water to cool down and stop the cooking. Use your hands to squeeze as much excess water as you can from the spinach. This is a key step so the gyoza doesn't become watery. Transfer the spinach to a cutting board and finely chop it. Set aside.

Place the tofu on a clean kitchen towel or large cheesecloth. Roll up the cloth and wring, like you're wringing dry a wet towel, to crumble the tofu and expel water from it.

Add the spinach, tofu, shiitake, garlic, ginger, scallion, miso, pine nuts, 1 tablespoon of the sesame oil, sugar, and *katakuriko* to a large bowl. Use your hands to mix the ingredients together for about 2 minutes. Mash and mush the mixture together, squeezing it through your fingers, so it turns into a sticky filling that will hold together when you spoon it into a dumpling skin.

To make the dumplings, prepare a tray by lightly dusting it with *katakuriko*. Place a gyoza skin in the palm of one hand with the floured side down. Dip a finger in the *katakuriko* mixed with warm water and wet the entire edge of the skin. This water-starch mixture is the "glue" that will hold the skin closed. Add about 1/2 to 3/4 tablespoon of the filling to the center of the skin. Use the index fingers and thumbs of both hands to fold the skin and pinch it together. See "How to Fold Gyoza" (page 32) for step-by-step instructions with photographs. Place completed gyoza on the tray, fold side up. Repeat until you've used up all the filling.

To cook the gyoza, preheat a nonstick pan or cast-iron skillet over high heat for about 5 minutes. (We like to use a 12-inch-diameter skillet with a cover to prepare gyoza.) When the skillet is hot, add 1 tablespoon of the sesame oil, making sure the entire surface is coated (you can use a wadded-up paper towel to carefully spread the oil). Begin adding the gyoza, one at a time, in neat rows, with the seam side up. A 12-inch skillet will hold about 20 gyoza. Once all the gyoza are added, fry them for about 10 seconds. Now quickly pour in the 2/3 cup of water over the gyoza and cover the skillet tightly. Cook over high heat for about 4 minutes. Uncover the skillet; there should be little or no water remaining. Cook for 1 minute more. Drizzle the remaining 1 tablespoon sesame oil over the gyoza and cook for an additional 1 minute, for about 6 minutes total cooking time. The gyoza should look glossy with the skins cooked through. Turn off the heat and use a thin fish spatula to transfer the gyoza to a serving plate, this time with the seam side down (you want to show off the beautifully crispy, browned bottoms of the dumplings). Serve the dumplings steaming hot, with the dipping sauce on the side. Dip in the sauce to eat.

Gyoza

3 CURRY

CURRY

It seems that everybody in Japan absolutely loves curry. Long the go-to favorite food in school cafeterias, restaurants, and home kitchens, it's savored from one end of the archipelago to the other. But curry doesn't sound exactly, er, Japanese. What's going on?

Curry, you surmise correctly, originated on the Indian subcontinent. But that curry—the one prepared from fresh spices and aromatics—is not what first arrived in Japan. In the 1870s, it was British-style curry powder, the C&B brand to be exact, that was introduced to the country, and it was originally considered a European food, not an Asian one. The first dishes cooked with this curry powder in Japan are said to have involved oysters and red frog. They weren't exactly a hit. It wasn't until the early twentieth century, when curry was adopted by the Japanese navy (see "Kaigun Curry—the Curry of the Japanese Navy," page 50), and especially the army (where ordinary soldiers take turns cooking, as opposed to mess cooks on a ship), that this dish started filling the bellies—and capturing the hearts—of Japanese. When sailors and soldiers returned home, they brought their beloved curry with them, and before long the dish became wildly popular and enduringly beloved.

So what exactly is Japanese-style curry?

When the English version was first introduced to the country, it was a soupy concoction meant to be sopped up with bread. The Japanese adopted the dish to their tastes, first by thickening it so it could be eaten more easily with their staple starch—rice. Then they added familiar ingredients, so Japanese curry began to resemble homey dishes like *niku jaga*, a stew of beef and root vegetables.

In classic Japanese curry (or *karé*, as it's pronounced in Japan), you'll always find carrots, onions, and potatoes, but also apples or sometimes other fruits to add sweetness. Besides being sweeter, Japanese curry isn't nearly as hot as Indian curry. It's always eaten with rice. And even in a land of chopsticks, it is always eaten with a Western-style spoon.

If you visit a hundred homes in Japan, you'll find a hundred styles of curry—it's the ultimately customizable dish. While the classic version is made with beef, curry is now cooked with pork, chicken, lamb, fish, just vegetables, you name it. Different cities, towns, and regions in Japan have their own favorite curries, often reflecting prized local ingredients. The citizens of Kumamoto are proud of their local horse meat curry, for example, while squid ink curry is enjoyed in Hokkaido, and an oyster version in Hiroshima. The list goes on.

Japanese curry can now be prepared quickly with cubes of instant roux you can buy at any Asian market here in America. But—as with all processed foods—we avoid those artificially flavored, stabilizer- and other junk-impregnated cubes. Why not make curry from scratch, like we do? The taste is incomparable, it's easy, and you can freeze the leftovers. Once you sample the curries in this chapter, we know you'll become a believer, too.

In the recipes that follow, we start with old-school retro curry, then introduce more contemporary versions and even throw in an authentic battleship's recipe. When cooking these dishes, we encourage you to experiment—add more spices and herbs or vary ingredients. Go crazy, conjure up your very own special curry. Just be sure to send us the recipe.

RETRO CURRY

Let's dial it back to where it all began: old-school Japanese curry. Sweet-savory, fragrant, rich—and irresistible—this dish calls for the classic Japanese curry ingredients, that is, root vegetables, apple, and beef. And you thicken it using an old-fashioned roux, a French-style thickening agent for sauces made by cooking together butter and flour (a testament to this particular curry's Western roots). We use S&B curry powder, a Japanese brand founded in the 1920s and widely available in Asian markets here, but you can also substitute with Madras curry (usually sold in cans in supermarkets) or any curry powder you like. You can riff on this basic recipe in endless ways. Use chicken, pork, or seafood instead of beef. Add other vegetables: celery, eggplant, green pepper, daikon, broccoli, spinach, or tomato wedges (add the tomato 10 minutes before finishing so it doesn't break down). Use honey or even mango to sweeten the curry. Or throw the onions in at the beginning, with the beef, and totally brown them (like Tadashi does in his lamb curry, page 52), which will both help thicken the dish and add more intensely caramel flavors. Experiment and have fun.

1 pound stew beef (or any cut of beef you desire), cut into bite-size cubes

2 teaspoons salt

1/2 teaspoon pepper

6 tablespoons butter

1 pound medium onions (about 3), peeled and coarsely chopped

8 ounces carrots (about 2 medium carrots), cut rangiri style (see page 48)

1 tablespoon grated ginger (about 1/3 ounce)

1 teaspoon grated garlic (about 2 cloves, peeled and grated)

1 large apple (about 8 ounces), peeled and grated

5 cups beef stock

3 tablespoons flour

2 tablespoons curry powder

2 tablespoons garam masala, an aromatic Indian spice mixture (or substitute with curry powder)

3/4 pound potatoes, peeled and cut into bite-size pieces

Steamed rice, for serving

Season the beef with 1 teaspoon of the salt and the pepper. Melt 2 tablespoons of the butter in a large pot over medium heat. Add the beef and cook, stirring frequently, for about 2 minutes, until the meat browns (to lock in the flavor). Add the onion, and cook, stirring constantly, for about 5 minutes, until the onion begins to turn translucent. Add the carrots, ginger, and garlic, and cook and stir for 2 more minutes. Add the apple, stock, and remaining 1 teaspoon of the salt. Reduce the heat to low, cover, and simmer for 1 hour.

While the ingredients are simmering, prepare the roux. Melt the remaining

4 tablespoons butter in a small saucepan over low heat. Add the flour, stirring constantly for about 3 minutes. The flour will first bind to the butter, then the mixture will break apart, and look like large blonde crumbs. At this point, add the curry powder and garam masala and stir for 2 more minutes, until the roux releases a heady, toasted curry fragrance. Remove the saucepan from the heat and set aside.

Once the ingredients have simmered for 1 hour, add the potatoes. (Add 1/2 cup of water at this point if the curry seems too dry; it should have the consistency of gravy.) Scoop a ladleful of liquid from the

continued >

Curry

47

pot and add it to the roux, mixing together to create a paste. Add the roux paste to the large pot and mix well. Simmer for 20 more minutes, or until the potatoes are tender. Mix frequently, scraping the curry from the bottom of the pot, being careful not to burn. When the curry is ready, serve with steamed white rice.

How to Cut *Rangiri* Style

Rangiri is a handy Japanese cutting technique to create uniform pieces from unevenly sized roots like carrots, lotus, or burdock. This method also creates a lot of surface area on cut pieces, so they cook faster and absorb flavors better. The key to this technique is rolling the ingredient while you cut. Here's how you do it: Cut a root on an angle, roll a quarter turn, cut on an angle. Repeat until you've cut up the entire root.

BATTLESHIP CURRY

This is the curry served every Friday aboard the Japanese naval patrol ship *Hachijo* (see page 50), which we adapted for four, instead of four hundred! We love the curry creativity of Japanese navy cooks. Check out the ingredients in this version: cheese, honey, ketchup, a hit of strong coffee—the last one, we guess, to keep sailors extra alert when the Klaxon blares! When we cooked it up, we were surprised how tasty and complex it came out. The cheese melts into the curry, adding another layer of flavor, and thickening it, too. Add more pork if you like your curry meatier; Japanese cooks usually go lighter on the protein. And don't forget, navy curry isn't navy curry without salad on the side and a glass of milk (see page 50).

SERVES 4, WITH LEFTOVERS

1 pound boneless pork shoulder, cut into bite-size cubes

1 teaspoon salt

1 teaspoon pepper

2 tablespoons vegetable oil

1 tablespoon butter

1 pound medium onions (about 3), peeled and coarsely chopped

3 cloves garlic, thinly sliced

8 ounces carrots (about 2 medium carrots), cut rangiri style (see opposite)

5 cups torigara stock (page 25) or water

5 tablespoons curry powder

3 tablespoons tonkatsu sauce, store-bought or homemade (page 62)

2 tablespoons Japanese Worcestershire sauce (see page 234)

1/2 teaspoon ichimi togarashi (see page 235), or 1/4 teaspoon cayenne

2 teaspoons honey

2 tablespoons ketchup

2 medium Idaho potatoes (about 2/3 pound), peeled, cubed, and placed in bowl of water

1 tablespoon katakuriko (potato starch)

1 tablespoon water

1 cup grated Parmesan cheese (about 2 ounces)

1/2 cup grated mild Cheddar cheese (about 4 ounces)

1/2 cup brewed black coffee

Steamed rice, for serving

Season the pork with the salt and 1/2 teaspoon of the pepper. Preheat a large pot over high heat. Add the oil and butter. When the butter has melted, add the pork. Cook, stirring frequently, for about 2 minutes, until the exterior of the pork turns white. Add the onions, and cook, stirring constantly, for 2 minutes. Add the garlic and carrots and cook and stir for 2 minutes more.

Add the stock to the pot. When the liquid boils, reduce the heat to low and add the curry powder, tonkatsu sauce, Worcestershire sauce, remaining 1/2 teaspoon black pepper, *ichimi toragarshi*, honey, and ketchup. Mix well to combine the seasonings. Cover and simmer for 30 minutes, mixing occasionally.

continued >

Curry

Add the potatoes to the pot, cover, and simmer for 15 minutes. While the curry is simmering, mix together the *katakuriko* with the water in a small bowl.

Add the Parmesan cheese, Cheddar cheese, coffee, and *katakuriko* mixture to

the pot. Simmer for 5 minutes more, mixing occasionally.

Serve with steamed white rice, a side salad (see below), and a glass of milk.

Kaigun Curry—the Curry of the Japanese Navy

How do you feed a ship full of hungry sailors quickly, efficiently—and deliciously? For more than a hundred years, the Japanese navy's answer has been to rely on, yep, you guessed it, curry.

The Japanese navy first learned about curry from English seamen—some of whom served as advisers in Japan—because the British navy regularly served this food on their ships. Curry quickly caught on among Japanese sailors and became a much-anticipated Friday tradition aboard ship, the day when the mess would whip up massive batches of the dish (and we mean massive—picture a cement mixer and you'll get an idea of the size of a typical ship-board cooking pot). The Friday curry meal habit continues to this day, with each ship in the navy proud of its own custom version. In fact, on the official Japanese Defense Forces website, we found curry recipes from dozens of ships, employing ingredients as varied (and sometimes flat-out odd) as red wine, instant coffee, chocolate, blueberry jam, cheese, peaches, heavy cream, and pickles. The ships compete with each other in curry contests, and the naval base of Yokosuka (near Tokyo) holds an annual curry festival attended by thousands of sailors and civilians alike.

But while the curries vary from ship to ship, one thing remains constant. No matter what the vessel, Japanese navy curry is always served with rice; a "side salad" of tomatoes, lettuce, and boiled egg; and a nice, tall glass of whole milk—a well-balanced nutritional combo dreamed up by intrepid military dietitians, and one that sailors love.

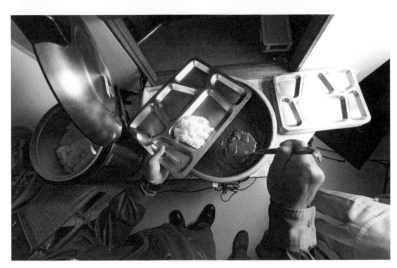

TADASHI'S LAMB CURRY

Tadashi whipped up this version for his lamb-loving family a few years ago, and they still haven't stopped raving about it. In this contemporary style of curry, you'll notice there's no roux—slow-cooking the onions is the secret to thickening it. So be sure to sauté the onions until they're really browned and "melt" into the stock. Not only do the onions thicken, but when cooked this way, they also release a sublime sweetness to the dish and a layer of beautiful toasty flavor, which works so nicely with the lamb. The wine, tomato, ginger, thyme, and other flavorings add even more complexity.

1 pound lamb shoulder, cut into bite-size cubes

1 1/2 teaspoons salt

1/2 teaspoon pepper

2 teaspoons garam masala

1 tablespoon vegetable oil

2 tablespoons butter

2 pounds medium onions (about 5 or 6), peeled, cut in half lengthwise, and thinly sliced against the grain

8 ounces carrots (about 2 medium), peeled and thinly sliced

2 stalks celery (about 4 ounces), thinly sliced

5 cloves garlic, peeled and thinly sliced

6 tablespoons curry powder

2 cups dry white wine

4 cups water

5 sprigs fresh thyme

1 bay leaf

1 pound tomatoes, coarsely chopped

1 tablespoon tomato paste

1 teaspoon grated ginger

1 tablespoon brown sugar

2 tablespoons soy sauce

1/2 teaspoon ichimi togarashi (see page 235), or 1/4 teaspoon cayenne pepper

Steamed rice, for serving

Season the lamb with 1 teaspoon of the salt, pepper, and garam masala. Preheat a large pot over high heat. Add the oil and butter. When the butter has melted, add the lamb. Cook the lamb, stirring frequently, for about 3 minutes, until the meat browns. Transfer the meat to a plate and set aside.

Reduce the heat to medium and add the onions to the pot. Cook for about 15 minutes, or until the onions soften and brown. Stir occasionally; be careful that the onions don't burn. Add the carrots, celery, and garlic and cook for about 5 more minutes, stirring occasionally, until the vegetables begin to turn translucent. Add 3 tablespoons of the curry powder and cook, stirring frequently, for about 1 minute. Add the wine and cook for 1 minute. Add the water, thyme, bay leaf, tomatoes, tomato paste, and ginger, and mix to combine. Reduce the heat to low, cover, and simmer for 30 minutes, stirring occasionally.

Add the brown sugar, soy sauce, remaining 1/2 teaspoon salt, *ichimi togarashi*, and remaining 3 tablespoons curry powder to the pot. Stir for about 1 minute to combine the ingredients. Cover again and simmer for 30 minutes more. Serve with steamed white rice.

Other Dishes You Can Make with Curry

So you whipped up a monster batch of mouthwatering Japanese curry. Nice! Now, what to do with leftovers? If you're like us, you'll freeze single-portion-sizes of curry (in plastic storage containers or zip-top storage bags) to reheat in a hurry. Or, you can use your curry to create other dishes. Classic examples include curry udon (page 183), katsukaré (slather curry over the tonkatsu on page 65), and karédon (follow the curry udon recipe on page 183, but pour over rice instead of noodles, donburi style). Be sure to try them all.

Curry Condiments

As we describe on page 44, rice on the side is mandatory for Japanese curry (and don't forget that spoon). Many Japanese also can't imagine enjoying curry without one, or both, of these classic condiments: *fukujin-zuke* and *rakkyo*. *Fukujin-zuke* is a bright red, sweet-savory pickle made from a mixture of cucumber, daikon, and ginger that has been marinated in soy sauce, sake, sugar, and other traditional seasonings. *Rakkyo* is a Japanese-style shallot that's been pickled in sweet vinegar; it's a crunchy, tangy, and refreshing condiment. Both can be found in Japanese markets.

WAFU SEAFOOD CURRY

Wafu means "Japanese style," in this case, the ingredients of the curry. Here, classic Japanese seasonings like dashi, soy sauce, sake, and mirin create the flavor to match the seafood in the dish. And what's more Japanese style than seafood? The result is a delicate, heavenly curry, this one thickened with *katakuriko*, or potato starch, a fundamental Japanese technique. Besides rice, this curry is fantastic when served over udon noodles.

SERVES 4

8 ounces sea scallops (10/20 size)

8 ounces squid, cleaned and cut into ¼-inch slices (tentacles are great, too)

8 ounces small shrimp, cleaned, shelled, and deveined

½ teaspoon salt

¼ teaspoon white pepper

2 tablespoons toasted sesame oil

1 medium Spanish onion (about 12 ounces), cut into ¼-inch slices

2 cloves garlic, sliced

1½ medium carrots (about 6 ounces), cut on an angle into ¼-inch slices

4 tablespoons curry powder

¼ cup sake

¼ cup mirin

4 ounces shiitake mushrooms (about 8), stemmed and cut into ¼-inch slices

4 cups dashi (page 161)

½ cup soy sauce

1 tablespoon sugar

3 tablespoons katakuriko (potato starch) dissolved in 3 tablespoons water

2 scallions (about 2 ounces), trimmed and thinly sliced on an angle

Steamed rice, for serving

Add the scallops, squid, shrimp, salt, and pepper to a bowl and gently toss to coat the seafood. Set aside.

Heat the sesame oil in a large pot over high heat. Add the onion and cook, stirring constantly, for about 1 minute. Add the garlic and carrots, and cook, stirring constantly, for about 2 minutes. Add the seafood mixture and cook, stirring constantly, for about 1 minute. Add 3 tablespoons of the curry and cook, stirring constantly, for about 30 seconds. Add the sake and mirin and cook, stirring, for about 1 minute.

Add the shiitake, dashi, soy sauce, and sugar, and mix to combine. When the liquid boils, reduce the heat to a simmer and cook, stirring occasionally, for about 2 minutes. As the curry cooks, remove any scum that appears on the surface. Add the remaining 1 tablespoon curry and stir to combine. Cook for about 2 minutes more. Increase the heat to medium-high and add the *katakuriko*-water mixture. Cook, stirring constantly, for about 1 minute to thicken the curry. Turn off the heat and serve, garnishing with the scallions. Eat with steamed white rice on the side.

MISO CURRY

Tadashi created this bold, unforgettable beef curry with a dynamic duo of beautiful artisan miso—*Hatcho* and *Sendai*—to give it a serious umami-laden wallop, which marries perfectly with the meat. *Hatcho* is a dense, intense, chocolate-colored miso with an almost meaty savoriness. *Sendai* is a rustic "countryside"-style, aged miso that we just love. You can usually find these in Japanese markets. But if not, substitute any good, aged *aka* miso (red miso), and you'll still get great results. (Also, sometimes it's easier to find *aka* dashi, which is *Hatcho* miso cut with *shiro* miso [white miso], instead of *Hatcho*.) Also, one cooking note: be sure to keep the burdock soaking in water until you use it, so it doesn't turn brown.

6 cups torigara stock (page 25), or 6 cups water mixed with 2 tablespoons torigara base

¼ cup Hatcho miso (see page 234)

2 tablespoons Sendai miso (see page 234)

2 tablespoons sugar

1 pound beef (any cut is fine, like stew meat or even sirloin), cut into 1-inch cubes

1 teaspoon salt

1 teaspoon ground black pepper

1 tablespoon vegetable oil

1 tablespoon butter

1 medium Spanish onion (about 12 ounces), peeled and sliced

2 cloves garlic, peeled and coarsely chopped

1 medium carrot (about 4 ounces), peeled and sliced

6 ounces daikon, peeled and cut into pieces rangiri style (see page 48)

4 ounces burdock root, skin scraped and cut into pieces rangiri style (see page 48)

5 tablespoons curry powder

2 tablespoons flour

1 cup red wine

Steamed rice, for serving

Add the *torigara* stock, *Hatcho* miso, *Sendai* miso, and sugar to the work bowl of a blender. Pulse for about 1 minute, until smooth. Set aside.

Season the beef with the salt and ½ teaspoon of the ground black pepper.

Heat the oil and butter in a large saucepan over high heat. When the butter melts, add the beef and cook, stirring constantly, for about 1 minute, until the meat browns. Be sure to turn each cube of beef so they all brown. Add the onion and garlic and cook, stirring constantly, for about 2 minutes, until the onion becomes translucent. Add the carrot and daikon and cook, stirring constantly, for about 30 seconds. Add the burdock root and cook, stirring constantly, for about 30 seconds. Add 3 tablespoons of the curry and cook for about 30 seconds. Add the flour and cook, stirring constantly, for 30 seconds. Add the wine and cook, stirring constantly, for about 30 seconds.

Add the *torigara*-miso mixture and stir to combine. When the liquid comes to a boil, reduce the heat to a simmer and cook for about 45 minutes, until the liquid reduces by about half. Add the remaining 2 tablespoons curry and the remaining ½ teaspoon black pepper, stirring to combine. Simmer for 15 minutes more. Serve with steamed white rice.

Curry

SAPPORO SOUP CURRY

Okay, so a hundred-plus years after Japan discovered loose, soupy British-style curry and thickened and adapted it for a rice-eating culture, guess what? Soup curry makes a comeback! This second coming, as it were, began in 1971 when a restaurant in cold, snowy Sapporo, on the northern main island of Hokkaido, whipped up a comforting, soupy "medicine curry," loaded with spices and herbs. Twenty years later, another Sapporo joint, named Magic Spice, picked up this curry, but minus the medicinals. They dubbed it, simply, "soup curry" and the effect was indeed magical—before long this tasty curry spread and specialized soup curry restaurants began popping up all over the city. Lucky for us: this lighter curry, loaded with veggies and chicken, is an absolute delight. But soupy or not, you still eat it with rice.

SERVES 4

6 ounces Japanese or Chinese eggplant (about 2 small eggplants)

8 ounces zucchini (about 1 large zucchini)

8 ounces red pepper (about 1 large red pepper), cored

2 tablespoons vegetable oil

1 medium Spanish onion (about 12 ounces), peeled and cut into small dice

1¼ medium carrots (about 5 ounces), peeled and cut into small dice

1 teaspoon finely chopped garlic

1 teaspoon finely chopped ginger

4 chicken legs, boned and cut into 1-inch-wide slices (about 1¾ pounds chicken after boning)

4 tablespoons curry powder

6 cups torigara stock (page 25), or 6 cups water mixed with 2 tablespoons torigara base

2 teaspoons salt

2 bay leaves

2 whole dried Japanese chilies (takano tsume)

3 tablespoons olive oil

Steamed rice, for serving

Cut the eggplant and zucchini in half lengthwise, and slice the halves on an angle into about 3-inch-long pieces. Cut the red pepper in half lengthwise, and cut into 1-inch-thick lengthwise strips. Set the vegetables aside.

Heat the vegetable oil in a large saucepan over high heat. Add the onion, carrot, garlic, and ginger and cook, stirring constantly, for about 3 minutes, until the onion turns translucent. Add the chicken and cook, stirring constantly, until the meat turns white. Add the curry powder and cook, stirring constantly, for 1 minute. Add the *torigara* stock, salt, bay leaves, and Japanese chilies and stir to combine. When the liquid comes to a boil, reduce the heat to a simmer. Cook the curry for about 7 minutes, stirring occasionally. Remove any scum that appears on the surface.

While the curry is simmering, heat the olive oil in a large skillet over high heat. Add the eggplant, zucchini, and red pepper, and cook, stirring constantly, for about 2 minutes, until the vegetables soften. Remove from the heat.

Once the curry has cooked for 7 minutes, add the sautéed eggplant, zucchini, and red pepper, and stir to combine. Cook for about 5 minutes more, stirring occasionally, until the vegetables are cooked through. As the curry cooks, remove any scum or excess oil that appears on the surface. Serve in soup bowls, with steamed white rice on the side.

4 TONKATSU

TONKATSU

Thank an inventive chef named Kida Motojiro for bequeathing to the world this dish of glistening pork fillets, breaded with delightfully crispy crumbs and dunked in bubbling hot oil until perfectly juicy, crunchy, and browned. In 1899, Chef Kida had an *ah-ha!* moment: Why not cook pork, which at the time was a newly popular *yoshoku*, or Western food (see page 206), dipped in batter and deep-fried just like classic Japanese tempura?

But instead of lacy tempura batter, the chef decided to coat thinly sliced pork with crunchy panko crumbs, an inspired idea. After he introduced the dish at his Western-style restaurant in Tokyo called Rengatei—which is still going strong—he continued to tinker with various cuts of pork and side dishes in an attempt to perfect it. By 1904, he settled on thinly sliced raw cabbage and a Japanese take on Worcestershire sauce as accompaniments, the very same pairings that we still use today.

Within a couple of decades, more and more restaurants in Tokyo adopted the dish, and started calling it tonkatsu—short for *tonkatsuletu,* which is Japanglish for "pork cutlet." By the 1930s, the name stuck, the cabbage and sauce accompaniments stuck, and a standard thickness of the pork loin stuck. A tonkatsu *boom-mu* (boom) took off across Japan and a new comfort food was born, savored both at home and in restaurants for more than a century and counting.

While original tonkatsu remains as popular as ever, over the years creative chefs and home cooks evolved the dish and developed mouthwatering new versions. In this chapter, we share some of our favorite tonkatsu dishes, from classic to contemporary.

HOMEMADE PANKO BREAD CRUMBS Master Recipe

While we don't expect you to bake bread using electric current like professional panko producers do (see below), you can still create an approximation of Japan's signature crumb at home by using Japanese-style white bread, called *shokupan*. This bread is similar to typical Wonderbread-like white bread, but *shokupan* seems to be fluffier (whether it's the flour or some kind of secret technology, we're not sure), which helps it become more flaky than crumby, à la panko.

MAKES ABOUT 2 CUPS

8 ounces Japanese-style sliced white bread, crusts removed

Arrange the bread slices in a single layer on a baking sheet or large tray. Allow the slices to dry at room temperature for 1 day. When the slices have dried, working in batches, crumble the bread into the work bowl of a food processor. Pulse for about 30 seconds, until the bread turns into large crumbs. Do not overprocess. You want the crumbs to look more like tiny bread flakes rather than like sawdust. Store in a tightly sealed container at room temperature. The crumbs will last for up to 3 months.

Panko Bread Crumbs

How do we get our tonkatsu, furai, and korokke to turn out so unbelievably crispy and crunchy—yet with a crust so unbelievably light and airy? Psst, here's the secret: panko, Japan's amazing bread crumb.

While run-of-the-mill bread crumbs are basically ground-up dried bread, panko is specially produced to turn out more like a coarse white flake than a crumb. The process begins with baking crustless white bread using electric current instead of an oven—a process invented in the early twentieth century—which gives panko its unique texture. Once the bread is air-dried, it's coarsely ground into the flakes. The result is a breadcrumb that stays crisp while deep-fried and absorbs very little oil, so ingredients coated in panko don't have the heaviness or greasiness usually associated with this cooking. Panko is the go-to crumb for Japanese cooking, but it's versatile enough to use in any dish that calls for bread crumbs. Look for panko crumbs without additives, preservatives, or other junk.

Tonkatsu

HOMEMADE TONKATSU SAUCE Master Recipe

The DIY ethos of our book gave Tadashi an inspiration: Why not create his own homemade version of tonkatsu sauce? With a bit of testing, tasting, and tinkering, he developed the mouthwatering recipe that follows. Like Bulldog sauce (see opposite), this tonkatsu sauce is a "Japanafied" evolution of what was originally a Western sauce (Worcestershire), so you'll find some unusual cross-cultural ingredient combinations here, like kombu and tomato paste, and soy sauce and bay leaf. And while we're both fans of Bulldog, we think you'll find Tadashi's version more complex, nuanced, and oh so sublime. So if you want to whip up something amazing, try making this sauce. You have to cook a large batch for the flavors to work, but you can keep extra sauce in the refrigerator for up to two weeks, or freeze it for up to two months.

MAKES ABOUT 7 CUPS

1 tablespoon vegetable oil

2 medium onions (about 1½ pounds), thinly sliced

2 medium apples (about 1 pound), peeled, cored, and coarsely chopped

1 pound tomatoes, coarsely chopped

3 cloves garlic, peeled and coarsely chopped

2 cups sake

3 cups water

2 teaspoons salt

¼ cup sugar

½ cup soy sauce

½ cup vinegar

1 tablespoon tomato paste

1 (6-inch) piece of kombu

1 bay leaf

Pinch cayenne (about ⅛ teaspoon)

Pinch ground white pepper (about ⅛ teaspoon)

Pinch cinnamon (about ⅛ teaspoon)

Pinch nutmeg (about ⅛ teaspoon)

Pinch allspice (about ⅛ teaspoon)

2 tablespoons Worcestershire sauce

Heat a large saucepan over medium heat. Add the oil. When the oil is hot, add the onions. Cook and stir for about 10 minutes, until the onions brown. Add the apples, tomatoes, garlic, sake, water, salt, sugar, soy sauce, vinegar, tomato paste, kombu, and bay leaf. Increase the heat to high. As soon as the liquid boils, reduce the heat to low and simmer for 30 minutes.

Remove the kombu and bay leaf, and allow the mixture to cool to room temperature. In batches, ladle the mixture into the work bowl of a blender or food processor. Blend until smooth, about 1 minute. Repeat until the entire mixture has been blended,

transferring the finished sauce to a large mixing bowl. Strain the sauce through a sieve or colander into a large saucepan, to remove bits of tomato skin and seeds (make sure the sieve or colander is not too fine, or the sauce won't strain). Discard the skin and seeds.

Add the cayenne, ground white pepper, cinnamon, nutmeg, allspice, and Worcestershire sauce to the sauce and mix well to combine. Transfer to a saucepan and simmer for 10 minutes over medium heat. Allow the sauce to return to room temperature before using.

MISO TONKATSU DIPPING SAUCE

Master Recipe

For a bit of variety, try this easy-to-prepare miso dipping sauce instead of classic tonkatsu sauce. Hailing from the miso-crazed city of Nagoya, it's lightly sweet and nicely balanced, and works with any tonkatsu dish in this chapter. In fact, in Nagoya, *miso-katsu*, tonkatsu slathered in miso sauce, is the standard rather than Bulldog.

MAKES ABOUT 2 CUPS

¼ cup sake

¼ cup mirin

¼ cup water

2 tablespoons sugar

¼ cup Hatcho miso or red miso (see page 234)

2 tablespoons ground toasted sesame

Add the sake, mirin, water, and sugar to a saucepan and place over medium heat. Simmer for about 3 minutes, then add the miso. Use a whisk to mix together the ingredients while they simmer. Remove from heat, add the ground sesame, and whisk until smooth. Allow the sauce to come to room temperature and serve.

Bulldog Sauce

To most Japanese, tonkatsu just isn't tonkatsu unless it's slathered in Bulldog sauce, an inseparable mustard-on-a-hot-dog kind of pairing that harks back more than a century. But how did this iconic Japanese condiment come to be named after a cute, smooshed-faced pooch?

Set your time machine to the 1880s, when *yoshoku*, Western-style cuisine, became the rage in Japan. Trying to figure out what to do with unfamiliar foreign ingredients like pork and beef, Japanese food makers began creating new sauces and condiments to go with them. In 1886, a producer by chance discovered classic British Worcestershire sauce and started marketing the condiment as "European soy sauce." Producers then created a Japanese version, adding purees of apples and tomatoes to make the sauce sweeter and thicker to appeal to local tastes. But it still took about a decade for it to catch on with the public.

One of the first companies to market the Japanese version of "European soy sauce" adopted the English bulldog, that iconic British symbol, of course, as its trademark. This symbol—and sauce—became so popular that the company eventually changed its own name to Bulldog. What hasn't changed is the sauce's tangy, irresistible, savory-sweet flavor, and its direct link to a nineteenth-century transformation in Japanese eating.

CLASSIC TONKATSU

Ladies and gentlemen, may we have your attention, please: for your gustatory pleasure and delight, we now present the star of this chapter, tonkatsu. Here it is, the classic method, which is so incredibly satisfying, and also so easy to whip up. In this recipe, Tadashi shares a family secret—coat the pork with flour and egg *twice*, which makes the tonkatsu even crunchier. (Old-school tonkatsu joints in Japan, by the way, often use lard instead of oil for frying, which makes the tonkatsu *even* crunchier, but we're sticking to oil and saving on the heart bypass surgery bills, thank you very much.) Be sure to use a deep-fry (or "candy") thermometer to gauge temperature while you deep-fry; the easiest way to screw up this dish is to fry the pork too hot or too cold. In Japan, they say you deep-fry the tonkatsu until it's the color of *kitsune*, that is, the golden brown hue of a fox. Serve the pork this way: sliced into strips, resting against a mound of shredded cabbage, slathered in tonkatsu sauce, and with a dab of sinus-clearing *karashi* mustard on the side. A bowl of steaming white rice on the side is also mandatory. Now, that's what we call a meal, about as elemental and comforting as it gets.

SERVES 4

¾ pound cabbage, cored

4 fillets boneless pork shoulder or pork loin (about 1 pound), about ¾ inch thick

Salt and ground black pepper

2 eggs

½ cup flour

2 cups panko crumbs

Vegetable oil for deep-frying

4 teaspoons Japanese karashi mustard (see page 234)

½ cup tonkatsu sauce, store-bought or homemade (page 62)

Steamed rice, for serving

Slice the cabbage as thinly as possible (you can use a mandoline or other slicer). Follow instructions in Ultra-Crunchy Cabbage (see page 67) and set aside.

To prepare the pork fillets, lay the fillets flat on a cutting board. Tap the fillets with the back edge of a kitchen knife (the edge opposite the blade) to dig notches into the meat. Turn the knife so the flat side is facing the fillets. Pound the meat with the knife's flat side about 6 to 8 times on each side of the pork to flatten the meat to about ½ inch thick. Cut ½-inch notches into the white fat of the fillets, which will prevent the fillet from curling when

frying. (Fat shrinks faster than the meat when deep-frying.) Season the fillets on both sides with salt and pepper. Transfer the prepared pork fillets to a plate.

Beat the eggs in a bowl and set aside. Prepare 4 plates. Pour the flour onto the first plate. Pour the beaten egg onto the second plate. Pour the panko onto the third plate. Leave the fourth plate empty for now (this plate will hold the breaded tonkatsu).

Place a cast-iron skillet on a burner. Fill the skillet with vegetable oil to a height of at least 1 inch. Attach a deep-fry (or

continued >

Tonkatsu

"candy") thermometer to the side of the skillet. On a work surface near the skillet, set up a tray lined with newspaper or paper towels to drain the cooked tonkatsu. Turn the heat on to high. Heat the oil to 340°F.

While the oil is heating, bread the fillets. First, dredge a fillet in flour on both sides and shake off excess flour. Second, dip the fillet into the egg, coating both sides. Third, repeat the process, dredging the pork in the flour again on both sides, then coating it again with egg on both sides. Finally, lay the fillet on the panko crumbs. Pile panko on top of the pork with your fingers, then gently press the panko onto the fillet with the palms of your hand so a generous layer of panko sticks to the fillet on both sides. Repeat with the other fillets, then place them on the empty plate you prepared earlier.

When the oil has heated to 340°F, carefully slide the fillets into the skillet. Depending on the size of the skillet, cook the tonkatsu in batches. Be careful not to overfill the skillet, which will lower the cooking temperature; use, at most, half of the surface area of the oil to cook. While the tonkatsu is cooking, check the oil temperature with a candy thermometer. Regulate the heat to maintain a constant 340°F oil temperature. If the oil is too hot, the tonkatsu will burn; if it is too low, the tonkatsu will come out soggy and greasy.

Cook the tonkatsu for about 4 minutes, turning once, until the fillets turn golden brown. When they're ready, transfer the fillets to the paper-lined plate to drain. If possible, stand the fillets on their edges, so they drain better (you can use a metal rack to accomplish this, if you have one).

Transfer the tonkatsu to a cutting board and slice into strips. For each serving, place the pork on a plate, along with a heap of sliced cabbage and a dab of mustard. Serve topped with about 2 tablespoons of tonkatsu sauce or serve the sauce on the side, as you prefer. Serve piping hot with steamed white rice on the side.

Other ways to eat tonkatsu Another delicious way to enjoy tonkatsu is to eat it as a sandwich (*tonkatsu-sando*, as they say). Lay a tonkatsu fillet on a slice of bread (in Japan they typically use spongy white bread, but use any bread or roll that strikes your fancy), pour tonkatsu sauce over the fillet, cover with another slice of bread, and you're set. Perfect for the lunch pail at school or work. Tonkatsu is also amazing cooked with eggs over a bowl of rice (see katsudon, page 147) or slathered with Japanese curry (page 43) instead of tonkatsu sauce. And finally, try substituting chicken for the pork to make torikatsu, the poultry version.

How to Slice Cabbage

1 Cut the cabbage in half from head to stem

2 Cut the halves once more to make quarters

3 Remove the stem by cutting each quarter at an angle

4 Slice the cabbage as thinly as possible

Ultra-Crunchy Cabbage

Unsung, perhaps, but a side of shredded cabbage plays a vital role in tonkatsu, serving as a light, refreshing, indispensable counterpoint to a glorious fillet of deep-fried pork. Not only that, but cabbage and tangy tonkatsu sauce, Bulldog or our own (page 62), is a delicious delight in its own right. Moreover, the cabbage helps you digest the rich, deep-fried pork. So serving cabbage with tonkatsu is a must. But to do it right, your cabbage must have one key quality above all: hardcore, *ultra* crunchiness. Limp leaves just won't cut it.

Turning an ordinary head of cabbage into crunchy goodness is a snap. The trick is soaking it in ice-cold water to firm it up. Here's how we do it: Cut a head of cabbage in half lengthwise (head to stem) and core it. Now slice the cabbage as thinly as possible with a sharp knife or mandoline. Pour cold water into a large bowl and dump a tray of ice cubes in it. Add the cabbage and let it soak in the ice water for about 10 minutes. Strain and serve (remove any errant ice cubes from the cabbage). The shredded cabbage will now be refreshed, firm, and beautifully crunchy, the way it's supposed to be.

Tonkatsu

ROLLED KATSU WITH YUZU KOSHO

Here is a contemporary version of tonkatsu that we love, where you first slather the pork with irresistible *yuzu kosho*. If you're not familiar with *yuzu kosho*, you need to be; it's one of our very favorite Japanese ingredients (which we use extensively in our book *The Japanese Grill*). A fiery, aromatic condiment made from cured *yuzu* citrus peel, chilies, and salt, it's a perfect match with pork, adding alluring heat and citrusy complexity. You can find it in Japanese markets. Use either thinly sliced fresh pork belly or shoulder for this dish (you can find thinly sliced pork at Japanese or Asian markets). Eat rolled katsu with cabbage and rice only; you don't need any sauce—the *yuzu kosho* does it all.

SERVES 4

¾ pound cabbage, cored

1 pound fresh pork belly or pork shoulder, thinly sliced

2 teaspoons green yuzu kosho (see page 236)

2 eggs

½ cup flour

2 cups panko crumbs

Vegetable oil for deep-frying

¼ cup chopped scallion (optional)

Steamed rice, for serving

Slice the cabbage as thinly as possible (you can use a mandoline or other slicer). Follow instructions in Ultra-Crunchy Cabbage (page 67) and set aside.

Divide the pork belly strips into 4 portions (about 4 ounces each). On a work surface, assemble each portion of the pork belly as follows: lay the strips one next to the other lengthwise, making sure that their edges overlap. Once they're laid out, the strips should be about 5 inches across. Spread about ½ teaspoon of the *yuzu kosho* on top of the pork belly. Roll up the pork belly strips to create a log with a layer of *yuzu kosho* inside (think of a jelly roll). Place the rolled-up portion on a plate and repeat this process with the other portions.

Beat the eggs in a bowl and set aside. Prepare 4 plates. Pour the flour onto the first plate. Pour the beaten egg onto the second plate. Pour the panko onto the third plate. Leave the fourth plate empty for now (this plate will hold the breaded rolled katsu).

Place a cast-iron skillet on a burner. Fill the skillet with vegetable oil to a height of at least 1 inch. Attach a deep-fry (or "candy") thermometer to the side of the skillet. On a work surface near the skillet, set up a tray lined with newspaper or paper towels to drain the cooked rolled katsu. Turn the heat on to high. Heat the oil to 330°F.

While the oil is heating, bread the rolls. First, dredge a roll in flour on both sides and shake off the excess flour. Second, dip the roll into the egg, coating both sides. Finally, lay the roll on the panko crumbs. Pile panko on top of the pork with your fingers, then gently press the panko onto the roll so a generous layer of panko sticks to the meat on both sides. Be careful to handle the rolled katsu gently so it doesn't fall apart. Repeat with the other rolls, and

continued >

place the completed rolls on the empty plate you prepared earlier.

When the oil has heated to 330°F, carefully slide the rolled katsu into the skillet. Depending on the size of the skillet, cook the pork in batches. Be careful not to overfill the skillet, which will lower the cooking temperature; use at most half of the surface area of the oil to cook. While the rolled katsu is cooking, check the oil temperature with a candy thermometer. Regulate the heat to maintain a constant 330°F oil temperature. If the oil is too hot, the rolls will burn; if too low, they will come out soggy and greasy.

Cook the rolled katsu for about 8 minutes, turning once, until the rolls turn golden brown. When they're ready, transfer the

rolls to the paper-lined plate to drain. If possible, stand the rolls on their bottoms, so they drain better (you can use a metal rack to accomplish this, if you have one).

Transfer the rolled katsu to a cutting board and slice into bite-size pieces. For each serving, place a sliced roll on a plate, along with a heap of sliced cabbage. Sprinkle with about 1 tablespoon of the scallion. Serve piping hot with steamed white rice on the side.

Variations You can cook rolled katsu with a variety of Japanese condiments and seasonings. Try substituting the *yuzu kosho* with wasabi, *karashi* mustard, *sansho* powder, curry powder, or *shichimi togarashi*.

WARAJI KATSU

Waraji means "snowshoes" in Japanese, and the name is apt: this version of tonkatsu is paper-thin and almost spills over the plate. Why paper-thin? This dish originated in an old section of Tokyo called Kanda, which was home to many students. It was inexpensive, but it looked filling because of its gigantic size. Like students everywhere, Japanese undergrads craved cheap, satisfying chow, and the dish became a hit. In fact, Tadashi worked near Kanda as a teenager and regularly beelined to its waraji katsu joints to top off his tank.

SERVES 4

¾ **pound cabbage, cored**

4 **fillets boneless pork shoulder or pork loin (about 1 pound), about ¼ inch thick**

Salt and ground black pepper

2 **eggs**

½ **cup flour**

2 **cups panko crumbs**

Vegetable oil for deep-frying

4 **teaspoons Japanese karashi mustard (see page 234)**

½ **cup tonkatsu sauce, store-bought or homemade (page 62)**

Steamed rice, for serving

Slice the cabbage as thinly as possible (you can use a mandoline or other slicer). Follow instructions in Ultra-Crunchy Cabbage (page 67) and set aside.

To prepare the pork fillets, lay the fillets flat on a cutting board. Tap the fillets with the back edge of a kitchen knife (the edge opposite the blade) to dig notches into the meat. Turn the knife so the flat side is facing the fillets. Pound the meat with the knife's flat side to about $1/8$ inch thickness, like veal scaloppini. Cut $1/2$-inch notches into the white fat of the fillets, which will prevent the fillet from curling when frying. (Fat shrinks faster than the meat when deep-frying.) Season the fillets with salt and pepper on one side only (sufficient seasoning for this thin fillet). Transfer the prepared pork fillets to a plate.

Beat the eggs in a bowl and set aside. Prepare 4 plates. Pour the flour onto the first plate. Pour the beaten egg onto the second plate. Pour the panko onto the third plate. Leave the fourth plate empty for now (this plate will hold the breaded waraji katsu).

Use a cast-iron skillet large enough to fit the waraji katsu fillet. Place the skillet on a burner and fill it with vegetable oil to a height of at least 1 inch. Attach a deep-fry (or "candy") thermometer to the side of the skillet. On a work surface near the skillet, set up a tray lined with newspaper or paper towels to drain the cooked tonkatsu. Turn the heat on to high. Heat the oil to 350°F.

While the oil is heating, bread the fillets. First, dredge a fillet in flour on both sides and shake off the excess flour. Second, dip the fillet into the egg, coating both sides.

Third, lay the fillet on the panko crumbs. Pile panko on top of the pork with your fingers, then gently press the panko onto the fillet with the palms of your hand so a generous layer of panko sticks to the fillet on both sides. Repeat with the other fillets, placing them on the empty plate you prepared earlier.

Cook the waraji katsu one at a time, because they're so large. When the oil has heated to 350°F, carefully slide the first fillet into the skillet. While the tonkatsu is cooking, check the oil temperature with a candy thermometer. Regulate the heat to maintain a constant 350°F oil temperature. If the oil is too hot, the waraji katsu will burn; if too low, the waraji katsu will come out soggy and greasy.

Cook the waraji katsu for about 3 minutes, turning once, until the fillets turn golden brown. When they're ready, transfer the fillets to the paper-lined plate to drain. If possible, stand the fillets on their edges, so they drain better (you can use a metal rack to accomplish this, if you have one).

Transfer the waraji katsu to a cutting board and slice into strips. For each serving, place the pork on a plate, along with a heap of sliced cabbage and a dab of mustard. Slather with about 2 tablespoons of tonkatsu sauce or serve the sauce on the side, as you prefer. Serve piping hot with steamed white rice on the side.

MENCHI KATSU

Now we turn to a different style of katsu, this one made with inexpensive ground beef. This dish originated at a Tokyo restaurant in the nineteenth century. The eatery's name has been lost to history (or at least to us), but their culinary brainchild lives on in this amazing—and economical—dish that's now a hit with home cooks. With menchi katsu you create a savory patty that you coat in panko and deep-fry. Sounds decadent? You got that right. The trick is to deep-fry the menchi katsu as soon as you form and coat it, or else it'll release liquid and get soggy. So this is a dish you prepare and cook *à la minute*, as they say in French cuisine, right before you eat it. Also, the oil temperature in this recipe is lower than for pork, so the ground beef doesn't burn. Serve menchi katsu the way you would classic tonkatsu—with tonkatsu sauce, *karashi* mustard, shredded cabbage, and the essential bowl of steaming white rice on the side. (Our miso dipping sauce, page 34, is also fantastic with menchi katsu.)

SERVES 4

¾ pound cabbage, cored

1 pound ground beef

1 medium onion (about ¾ pound), finely chopped

1 teaspoon salt

½ teaspoon black pepper

2 tablespoons ketchup

2 tablespoons soy sauce

2 eggs

½ cup flour

2 cups panko crumbs

Vegetable oil for deep-frying

4 teaspoons Japanese karashi mustard (see page 234)

½ cup tonkatsu sauce, store-bought or homemade (page 62)

Steamed rice, for serving

Slice the cabbage as thinly as possible (you can use a mandoline or other slicer). Follow instructions in Ultra-Crunchy Cabbage (page 67) and set aside.

Add the beef, onion, salt, pepper, ketchup, and soy sauce to a large bowl. Use your hands to mix the ingredients together for at least 2 minutes. Press the ingredients with your hands and squeeze them through your fingers; you want the meat mixture to become well blended and slightly sticky so it holds together while deep-frying.

Beat the eggs in a bowl and set aside. Prepare 4 plates. Pour the flour onto the first plate. Pour the beaten egg onto the second plate. Pour the panko onto the third plate. Leave the fourth plate empty for now (this plate will hold the breaded menchi katsu).

Divide the meat mixture into 8 portions, about 4 ounces each. Roll each portion into a ball, then flatten each ball into a patty so it looks like a hamburger patty. The patty should be about ¾ to 1 inch thick. The meat mixture will be soft, so be gentle forming and handling the patties so they don't break. Place the completed patties on a large plate and set aside.

Place a cast-iron skillet on a burner. Fill the skillet with vegetable oil to a height of at least 1 inch. Attach a deep-fry (or "candy") thermometer to the side of the skillet. On a work surface near the skillet, set up a tray lined with newspaper or paper towels to drain the cooked menchi katsu. Turn the heat on to high. Heat the oil to 330°F.

While the oil is heating, bread the patties First, dredge a patty in flour on both sides and shake off the excess flour. Second, dip the patty into the egg, coating both sides. Finally, lay the patty on the panko crumbs. Pile panko on top of the patty with your fingers, then gently press the panko onto the patty so a generous layer of panko sticks to the meat on both sides. Repeat with the other patties, and place the completed patties on the empty plate you prepared earlier.

When the oil has heated to 330°F, carefully slide the patties into the skillet. Depending on the size of the skillet, cook the menchi katsu in batches. Be careful not to overfill the skillet, which will lower the cooking temperature; use at most half of the surface area of the oil to cook. While the menchi katsu is cooking, check the oil temperature with a candy thermometer. Regulate the heat to maintain a constant 330°F oil temperature. If the oil is too hot, the patties will burn; if too low, they will come out soggy and greasy.

Cook the menchi katsu for about 7 minutes, turning once, until the patties turn golden brown. When they're ready, transfer the patties to the paper-lined plate to drain. If possible, stand the patties on their edges, so they drain better (you can use a metal rack to accomplish this, if you have one).

To serve, place 2 menchi katsu on a plate, along with a heap of sliced cabbage and a dab of mustard. Slather with about 2 tablespoons of tonkatsu sauce or serve the sauce on the side, as you prefer. Eat piping hot with steamed white rice on the side.

5 FURAI & KOROKKE

FURAI

Remember Kida Motojiru, the chef who invented tonkatsu back in the nineteenth century (see page 60)? Well, it seems Chef Kida wasn't one to rest on his laurels. Working at his restaurant Rengatei, in Tokyo's Ginza section (still in business since 1895), the chef cooked up a number of other tasty dishes that have since become Japanese comfort food standards. Case in point: furai. Chef Kida was apparently influenced by European deep-fried foods like the French *côtelette* (fillets of veal or pork that are breaded and fried) when he thought up this dish, adapting "Western-style tempura," as it was called back then, to Japanese tastes, that is, using seafood and vegetables. Like tonkatsu, furai is coated with light, airy panko (page 61) and usually served with crunchy cabbage (page 67) on the side. But this dish typically calls for tangy Japanese-style tartar sauce, which we share in the recipe on page 80 (although some people opt for good ol' tonkatsu sauce for furai, too; up to you). Don't forget, too, that in Japan furai is often paired with salads like Tomato Salada (page 80), Potato Salada (page 210), or Macaroni Salada (page 212), which offer a filling counterpoint and make for a complete meal.

IWASHI FURAI

Fresh sardines (*iwashi*) are delicious coated in panko and deep-fried, and popular in Japan both at home and at neighborhood eateries. Japanese love these oily fish, which are super flavorful, plentiful, economical, and good for you. Talk about a super fish. In fact, sardines are a signature fish of the Tokyo Bay area, where they've been caught for centuries. We frequent one tiny *izakaya* (eating pub) there that serves sardines thirty ways (including furai, of course), and has a mural of sardines painted on its outside wall. The love runs deep. To prepare the sardines, you first have to remove the spine with your fingers, a nifty trick that we explain below.

SERVES 4

8 sardines (about 1 pound), cleaned and gutted

¼ teaspoon salt

⅛ teaspoon pepper

1 cup flour

2 eggs, beaten

4 cups panko crumbs

Vegetable oil for deep-frying

½ cup Japanese-style tartar sauce (page 80)

To prepare the sardines, rinse them under cold, running water and blot dry with paper towels. Place your index finger inside the cavity of a sardine and run it along the spine, pressing on the spine to separate it from the flesh. Remove the spine, spread open the sardine to butterfly it, and place on a plate lined with paper towels. Lightly season with salt and pepper. Repeat with the remaining sardines.

Prepare 4 plates: one with the flour, one with the beaten egg, one with the panko, and the fourth empty for now.

Place a cast-iron skillet on a burner. Fill the skillet with vegetable oil to a height of at least 1 inch. Attach a deep-fry (or "candy") thermometer to the side of the skillet. On a work surface near the skillet, set up a tray lined with newspaper or paper towels to drain the cooked furai. Turn the heat on to high. Heat the oil to 340°F.

While the oil is heating, bread the sardines one at a time. First, dredge a sardine in flour on both sides and shake off the excess flour. Second, dip the sardine into the egg, coating both sides. Finally, lay the sardine on the panko crumbs. Pile panko on top of the sardine with your fingers, then gently press the panko onto the sardine so a generous layer of panko sticks on both sides. Place the completed sardine on the empty plate. Repeat with the remaining sardines.

When the oil has reached 340°F, carefully slide the sardines into the skillet in batches. Be careful not to overfill the skillet, which will lower the cooking temperature; use at most half of the surface area of the oil to deep-fry. While the sardines are cooking, check the oil temperature with a candy thermometer. Regulate the heat to maintain a constant 340°F oil temperature. If the oil is too hot, the sardines will burn; if too low, the sardines will come out soggy and greasy.

Cook the sardines for about 2 minutes, until they turn golden brown. When they're ready, transfer the sardines to the paper-lined plate to drain.

Serve immediately, with Japanese-style tartar sauce on the side.

Furai & Korokke

KAKI FURAI

Kaki is the Japanese word for "oyster." Coated in panko and deep-fried, these oysters taste amazing, and are lighter and crispier than typical breaded and fried oysters. In fact, this might seem surprising to raw oyster–loving America, but in the land of raw seafood that is Japan, oysters are usually eaten cooked, to better bring out their flavor. And when oysters are deep-fried, the flavors are locked in especially well, and the contrast between the crunchy coating and the tender oyster is a delight. The secret to preparing this dish is very carefully following the oyster preparation steps, which removes moisture from the mollusk and prevents it from exploding in the deep fryer. Kaki furai pairs beautifully with Ultra-Crunchy Cabbage (page 67) and a bowl of steaming white rice as a meal on its own.

SERVES 4

1 pound fresh oysters (about 16), shucked

1 teaspoon salt

2 cups boiling water

Pinch ground black pepper

1 cup flour

2 eggs, beaten

4 cups panko crumbs

Vegetable oil for deep-frying

$1/2$ cup Japanese-style tartar sauce (page 80)

To prepare the oysters, mix together the oysters with $1/2$ teaspoon of the salt and then carefully rinse them under cold, running water. See "How to Prepare Oysters" (opposite) for step-by-step instructions with photographs. Handle the oysters gently or they will break apart. Transfer the oysters to a bowl. Pour the boiling water over the oysters. After 10 seconds, strain the oysters in a colander and allow them to come to room temperature. (This parboiling process firms up the oysters, expels water from them, and removes sliminess.)

When the oysters have cooled, carefully lay them on a plate lined with paper towels. Gently blot the top of the oysters with more paper towels to remove excess water. Season the oysters with the remaining $1/2$ teaspoon salt and the pepper.

Prepare 4 plates. Pour the flour onto the first plate. Pour the beaten egg onto the second plate. Pour the panko onto the third plate. Leave the fourth plate empty for now (this plate will hold the breaded oysters).

Place a cast-iron skillet on a burner. Fill the skillet with vegetable oil to a height of at least 1 inch. Attach a deep-fry (or "candy") thermometer to the side of the skillet. On a work surface near the skillet, set up a tray lined with newspaper or paper towels to drain the cooked furai. Turn the heat on to high. Heat the oil to 350°F.

While the oil is heating, bread the oysters one at a time. First, dredge an oyster in flour on both sides and shake off the excess flour. Second, dip the oyster into the egg, coating both sides. Finally, lay the oyster on the panko crumbs. Pile panko on top of the oyster with your fingers, then gently press the panko onto the oyster so a generous layer of panko sticks on both sides. Be careful to handle the oyster very gently so it doesn't break apart. Place the completed oyster on the empty plate. Repeat with the remaining oysters.

When the oil has reached 350°F, carefully slide the oysters into the skillet. Deep-fry the oysters in batches. Be careful not to overfill the skillet, which will lower the cooking temperature; use at most half of the surface area of the oil to cook. While the oysters are cooking, check the oil temperature with a candy thermometer. Regulate the heat to maintain a constant

350°F oil temperature. If the oil is too hot, the oysters will burn; if too low, the oysters will come out soggy and greasy.

Cook the oysters quickly, for about 1 minute, until they turn golden brown. When they're ready, transfer the oysters to the paper-lined plate to drain.

Serve immediately, with Japanese-style tartar sauce on the side.

How to Prepare Oysters

1 Gently mix the oysters with the salt and rinse with cold water

2 Carefully pour boiling water over the oysters and wait 10 seconds

3 Strain the oysters with a colander and allow them to come to room temperature

4 Carefully transfer them to a towel-lined plate and blot dry

Furai & Korokke

Japanese-Style Tartar Sauce

This is the go-to sauce for furai dishes. It is similar to classic American tartar sauce, but the big difference is the mayo. Here we use Japanese Kewpie mayonnaise (page 132), an umami-rich version that has less oil and is looser and smoother than typical pasty, store-bought mayo, which gives the sauce more punch. You can also add classic Japanese accents to the tartar sauce, if you'd like. For example, you can substitute 2 tablespoons of chopped shiso leaves for the parsley. Or add 2 teaspoons of wasabi or 1 teaspoon of red yuzu kosho.

MAKES ABOUT 2 CUPS

6 tablespoons finely chopped onion

1 cup Kewpie mayonnaise (page 132)

2 eggs, hard-boiled, peeled, cooled, and finely chopped

1/2 teaspoon salt

Pinch pepper

8 ounces cornichon pickles, finely chopped

1 tablespoon capers (in vinegar), finely chopped

1 tablespoon finely chopped parsley

1 tablespoon lemon juice

Thoroughly mix together all the ingredients in a bowl. Place in the refrigerator for at least 1 hour (overnight is even better) for the flavors to mingle before serving. This tartar sauce will keep in the refrigerator for about 2 weeks.

Tomato Salada

Wait until summer and early autumn when you can find really beautiful, vine-ripened tomatoes to prepare this lovely salad. (Pictured opposite, at the lower left.) The dressing is fantastic with leafy greens, too.

SERVES 4

1/2 cup finely chopped onion

1 teaspoon grated ginger

1 tablespoon toasted sesame oil

1 tablespoon soy sauce

1 tablespoon vinegar

1 teaspoon sugar

1/2 teaspoon salt

Pinch ground black pepper

1 pound beefsteak tomatoes, sliced

To make the dressing, whisk together the onion, ginger, sesame oil, soy sauce, vinegar, sugar, salt, and pepper in a bowl, until the dressing is well combined. Arrange the tomatoes on 4 plates. Spoon the dressing over the tomatoes and serve.

A sampling of Japanese salads (clockwise from top left): traditional wakame and cucumbers, lettuce with ginger-carrot dressing (page 213), potato salada (page 210), and tomato salada (opposite)

EBI FURAI

Here's another furai favorite loved across Japan, this time using shrimp. Fried shrimp is irresistible in any cuisine, but what makes this furai special is, as with oysters (page 78), the super crispy but light panko coating. Resting the shrimp after packing on the panko keeps them nice and straight when they fry. Deep-fry these shrimp hot and fast. As with the oysters, this dish pairs beautifully with Ultra-Crunchy Cabbage (page 67), too.

SERVES 4

1 cup flour

2 eggs

1/2 cup milk

1 teaspoon salt

1/2 teaspoon pepper

4 cups panko crumbs

1 pound large shrimp (13/16 size, about 16), cleaned, shelled, tail left on

Vegetable oil for deep-frying

1/2 cup Japanese-style tartar sauce (page 80)

Mix together the flour, eggs, milk, salt, and pepper in a bowl until the mixture becomes a smooth batter.

Arrange the batter, a plate with the panko, and an empty plate (to hold the breaded shrimp) on a work surface. Now bread the shrimp, one at a time. Dip the shrimp into the batter and shake off any excess. Lay the shrimp in the panko. Pile panko on top of the shrimp with your fingers, then gently press the panko onto the shrimp so a generous layer of panko sticks to the shrimp on both sides. Place the completed shrimp on the empty plate. Repeat with the remaining shrimp.

When all the shrimp are breaded, allow them to rest for 30 minutes at room temperature so the batter binds with the panko. You can also bread the shrimp ahead of time and refrigerate, loosely covered, for up to 4 hours.

Place a cast-iron skillet on a burner. Fill the skillet with vegetable oil to a height of at least 1 inch. Attach a deep-fry (or "candy") thermometer to the side of the skillet. On a work surface near the skillet, set up a tray lined with newspaper or paper towels to drain the cooked furai. Turn the heat on to high. Heat the oil to 340°F.

Carefully slide the shrimp into the skillet. Deep-fry the shrimp in batches. Be careful not to overfill the skillet, which will lower the cooking temperature; use at most half of the surface area of the oil to cook. While the shrimp are cooking, check the oil temperature with a candy thermometer. Regulate the heat to maintain a constant 340°F oil temperature. If the oil is too hot, the shrimp will burn; if too low, the shrimp will come out soggy and greasy.

Cook the shrimp for about 2 minutes, until they turn golden brown and give off a sweet batter fragrance. When they're ready, transfer the shrimp to the paper-lined plate to drain.

Serve immediately, with Japanese-style tartar sauce on the side.

KOROKKE

Like the furai recipes, it didn't take long for another delectable deep-fried dish to take off in Japan, this one called korokke, the Japanese phonetic pronunciation of "croquette." The local interpretation of the original European import, a korokke is chopped-up meat, vegetables, or seafood, formed into a log or patty, coated in crumbs, and deep-fried until golden brown. In the Japanese version, the crumbs are airy crispy panko (page 61), like with tonkatsu, and the standard accompaniments are crunchy thinly sliced cabbage and tonkatsu sauce, also like with tonkatsu. (Japanese also sometimes eat korokke between slices of bread, as a sandwich.) While easy to cook at home, korokke in Japan are also commonly sold from stalls and, especially, in butcher shops. There are tons of varieties—potato, shrimp, pumpkin, the list goes on—but the trio that follow are the classics.

POTATO KOROKKE

This is the classic korokke: potatoes, meat, and cream, formed into a patty and deep-fried. So satisfying, with a pleasing crunchy crust and a rich, delicious filling. The trick is cooking the potatoes dry, so they don't add too much moisture to the korokke, which will cause it to fall apart while frying. So instead of steaming or boiling the spuds, we dry roast them in the oven. Also, feel free to substitute ground beef for the ground pork if you'd like.

SERVES 4

1 pound russet potatoes

2 tablespoons butter

¼ large Spanish onion (about 4 ounces), peeled and finely minced

8 ounces ground pork

2 tablespoons soy sauce

2 tablespoons sugar

Pinch ground black pepper

¼ cup heavy cream

1 cup flour

2 eggs, beaten

4 cups panko

Vegetable oil for deep-frying

1 cup tonkatsu sauce, store-bought or homemade (page 62)

Preheat the oven to 400°F. Arrange the potatoes on a sheet pan and bake for 20 minutes, until a knife goes through the potatoes easily. Remove from the oven and allow the potatoes to come to room temperature. (Alternatively, microwave

continued >

potatoes for about 10 minutes.) When the potatoes have cooled, peel and set aside.

Melt the butter in a saucepan over medium heat. Add the onion and cook, stirring constantly, for about 1 minute, until they turn translucent. Add the pork and cook, stirring constantly, for about 5 minutes, until the pork cooks through and any liquid in the skillet evaporates. Break apart the pork as you stir. When the pork is ready, transfer to a large mixing bowl.

Add the potatoes to the pork and mash together until just combined (a potato masher is ideal here, or use a large spoon). Add the soy sauce, sugar, and pepper and mash together. Add the heavy cream and mash until all the ingredients are just combined. Do not mash too much. You don't want the mixture to be too smooth; you want bits of potato to remain, to give texture. (Akin to chunky peanut butter rather than smooth peanut butter.)

Transfer the potato mixture to a sheet pan and spread it out to make a flat disk about 1/2 inch thick. Place in the refrigerator uncovered to cool and firm up for about 1 hour.

While the potato mixture is cooling, prepare 4 plates. Pour the flour onto the first plate. Pour the beaten egg onto the second plate. Pour the panko onto the third plate. Leave the fourth plate empty for now (this plate will hold the breaded korokke).

Place a cast-iron skillet on a burner. Fill the skillet with vegetable oil to a height of at least 1 inch. Attach a deep-fry (or "candy") thermometer to the side of the skillet. On a work surface near the skillet, set up a tray lined with newspaper or paper towels to drain the cooked korokke.

When the potato mixture is ready, remove from the refrigerator and cut into 8 even

pieces (about 4 ounces each). Form 8 korokke patties, one at a time. Wet your hands, then place one of the pieces of the cooled potato mixture onto your palm. With both hands, gently form it into a patty that resembles a hamburger patty. Do this quickly; if you handle the mixture too much it can get soft and break apart while frying. Repeat for the remaining patties.

Turn on the heat under the skillet to high. Heat the oil to 340°F.

While the oil is heating, bread the korokke patties one at a time. First, dredge a patty in flour on both sides and shake off the excess flour. Second, dip the patty into the egg, coating both sides. Finally, lay the patty on the panko crumbs. Pile panko on top of the korokke with your fingers, then gently press the panko onto the patty so a generous layer of panko sticks on both sides. Be careful to handle the korokke very gently so it doesn't break apart. Place the completed korokke on the empty plate. Repeat with the remaining patties.

When the oil has reached 340°F, carefully slide the korokke into the skillet. Deep-fry the korokke in batches. Be careful not to overfill the skillet, which will lower the cooking temperature; use, at most, half of the surface area of the oil to cook. While the korokke are cooking, check the oil temperature with a candy thermometer. Regulate the heat to maintain a constant 340°F oil temperature. If the oil is too hot, the korokke will burn; if too low, the korokke will come out soggy and greasy.

Cook the korokke for about 3 minutes, until they heat through and turn golden brown (they're already cooked inside). When they're ready, transfer the korokke to the paper-lined plate to drain.

Serve immediately, with tonkatsu sauce.

CURRY RICE KOROKKE

This version uses that good ol' Japanese staple, rice, to bind the ingredients, instead of Western-style potatoes or cream. Flavored with ever-popular curry, it's another top contender for the Korokke Crown. And, indeed, the curry does add a phenomenal pop to the rice filling (reminds you of curry chahan, page 202). Like Kani Cream Korokke (page 89), this is another korokke that you can eat with or without tonkatsu sauce, as you prefer.

SERVES 4

2 tablespoons butter

4 ounces onion, peeled and finely minced

1 medium carrot (about 4 ounces), finely chopped

2 cloves garlic, chopped

8 ounces ground beef

3 tablespoons curry powder

1 cup sake

1 tablespoon soy sauce

1 tablespoon mirin

½ teaspoon salt

½ cup water

2 cups cooked Japanese short-grain rice

½ teaspoon ground black pepper

1 cup flour

2 eggs, beaten

4 cups panko

Vegetable oil for deep-frying

1 cup tonkatsu sauce, store-bought or homemade (page 62; optional)

Melt the butter in a saucepan over medium heat. Add the onion, carrot, and garlic and cook, stirring constantly, for about 2 minutes, until the onions turn translucent. Add the beef and cook, stirring constantly, for about 2 minutes, until the beef cooks through. Break apart the beef as you stir. Add 2 tablespoons of the curry powder and cook, stirring constantly, for about 2 minutes, until it's well combined with the beef and you smell a rich curry fragrance. Be careful that the curry doesn't burn; scrape the bottom of the pot as you stir. Add the sake, soy sauce, mirin, and salt. When the mixture comes to boil, simmer for about 2 minutes, stirring frequently. Add the

water. When the mixture returns to a boil, simmer for about 2 minutes, stirring frequently. Add the rice, the remaining 1 tablespoon curry powder, and the black pepper and cook, stirring constantly, for about 3 minutes, until the excess liquid is absorbed or evaporates, and the mixture thickens into a paste and binds. Be careful not to burn the mixture as you cook; keep scraping the bottom of the pan.

Transfer the curry mixture to a sheet pan and spread it out to make a flat disk about ½ inch thick. Place in the refrigerator to cool and firm up for about 1 hour.

While the curry mixture is cooling, prepare 4 plates. Pour the flour onto the first

continued >

Furai & Korokke

plate. Pour the beaten egg onto the second plate. Pour the panko onto the third plate. Leave the fourth plate empty for now (this plate will hold the breaded korokke).

Place a cast-iron skillet on a burner. Fill the skillet with vegetable oil to a height of at least 1 inch. Attach a deep-fry (or "candy") thermometer to the side of the skillet. On a work surface near the skillet, set up a tray lined with newspaper or paper towels to drain the cooked korokke.

When the curry mixture is ready, remove from the refrigerator and cut into 16 even pieces (about 3 ounces each). Form 16 korokke logs, one at a time. Wet your hands, then place one of the pieces of the cooled curry mixture onto your palm. With both hands, gently form it into a log about 2 inches long. Do this quickly; if you handle the mixture too much it can get soft and break apart while frying. Repeat for the remaining logs.

Turn on the heat under the skillet to high. Heat the oil to 340°F.

While the oil is heating, bread the korokke logs one at a time. First, dredge a log in flour on both sides and shake off the excess flour. Second, dip the korokke into

the egg, coating both sides. Finally, lay the log on the panko crumbs. Pile panko on top of the korokke with your fingers, then gently press the panko onto the log so a generous layer of panko sticks on both sides. Be careful to handle the korokke very gently so it doesn't break apart. Place the completed korokke on the empty plate. Repeat with the remaining logs.

When the oil has reached 340°F, carefully slide the korokke into the skillet. Deep-fry the korokke in batches. Be careful not to overfill the skillet, which will lower the cooking temperature; use, at most, half of the surface area of the oil to cook. While the korokke are cooking, check the oil temperature with a candy thermometer. Regulate the heat to maintain a constant 340°F oil temperature. If the oil is too hot, the korokke will burn; if too low, the korokke will come out soggy and greasy.

Cook the korokke for about 3 minutes, until they heat through and turn golden brown (they're already cooked inside). When they're ready, transfer the korokke to the paper-lined plate to drain.

Serve immediately, with tonkatsu sauce, on the side.

KANI CREAM KOROKKE

One of the all-time favorites in Korokke Land, here succulent crab (*kani* in Japanese) is combined with what is essentially a savory béchamel sauce (*cream* in Japanglish) and formed into cute little logs for deep-frying. The insides come out so creamy and velvety—irresistible. Eat these korokke with tonkatsu sauce, or not, they're also fantastic just on their own.

SERVES 4

2 tablespoons butter

¼ large Spanish onion (about 4 ounces), peeled and thinly sliced

6 tablespoons plus 1 cup flour

2 cups whole milk

8 ounces crabmeat (canned is fine, about 1 cup)

1 teaspoon salt

½ teaspoon ground black pepper

2 eggs, beaten

4 cups panko

Vegetable oil for deep-frying

1 cup tonkatsu sauce, store-bought or homemade (page 62; optional)

Melt the butter in a saucepan over medium-low heat. Add the onions and cook, stirring frequently, for about 5 minutes, until the onions are cooked through and translucent. Make sure the onions remain clear and don't brown; you don't want them to caramelize. Add 6 tablespoons of the flour and cook, stirring constantly, for about 1 minute to combine with the onions. Add the milk slowly (about ¼ cup of milk at a time), and stir constantly. Adding the milk gradually helps it bind with the flour. Cook, whisking constantly, for about 5 minutes, until it becomes smooth and velvety. Be careful that the mixture doesn't burn; scrape the bottom of the pot as you whisk. Add the crabmeat, salt, and pepper and cook, stirring constantly, for about 5 minutes until the mixture thickens into a paste like smooth mashed potatoes, and you can smell the crab aroma. (If the crab is watery, you may have to cook a little longer to thicken.) Be careful not to burn the mixture as you cook; keep scraping the bottom of the pan.

Transfer the crab mixture to a sheet pan and spread it out to make a flat disk about ½ inch thick. Place in the refrigerator to cool and firm up for about 1 hour.

While the crab mixture is cooling, prepare 4 plates. Pour the remaining 1 cup flour onto the first plate. Pour the beaten egg onto the second plate. Pour the panko onto the third plate. Leave the fourth plate empty for now (this plate will hold the breaded korokke).

Place a cast-iron skillet on a burner. Fill the skillet with vegetable oil to a height of at least 1 inch. Attach a deep-fry (or "candy") thermometer to the side of the skillet. On a work surface near the skillet, set up a tray lined with newspaper or paper towels to drain the cooked korokke.

When the crab mixture is ready, remove from the refrigerator and cut into 16 even pieces (about 1½ ounces each). Form 16 korokke logs, one at a time. Wet your hands, then place one of the pieces of the cooled crab mixture onto your palm.

continued >

With both hands, gently form it into a log about 2 inches long. Do this quickly; if you handle the mixture too much it can get soft and break apart while frying. Repeat for the remaining logs.

Turn on the heat under the skillet to high. Heat the oil to 340°F.

While the oil is heating, bread the korokke logs one at a time. First, dredge a log in flour on both sides and shake off the excess flour. Second, dip the korokke into the egg, coating both sides. Finally, lay the log on the panko crumbs. Pile panko on top of the korokke with your fingers, then gently press the panko onto the log so a generous layer of panko sticks on both sides. Be careful to handle the korokke very gently so it doesn't break apart. Place the completed korokke on the empty plate. Repeat with the remaining logs.

When the oil has reached 340°F, carefully slide the korokke into the skillet. Deep-fry the korokke in batches. Be careful not to overfill the skillet, which will lower the cooking temperature; use, at most, half of the surface area of the oil to cook. While the korokke are cooking, check the oil temperature with a candy thermometer. Regulate the heat to maintain a constant 340°F oil temperature. If the oil is too hot, the korokke will burn; if too low, the korokke will come out soggy and greasy.

Cook the korokke for about 3 minutes, until they heat through and turn golden brown (they're already cooked inside). When they're ready, transfer the korokke to the paper-lined plate to drain.

Serve immediately, with tonkatsu sauce on the side.

6 KARA-AGE

KARA-AGE

Kara-age (pronounced "kara-ageh") is technique of Japanese deep-frying imported from China. Already known in Japan by the eighteenth century, kara-age differs from another popular deep-frying method, tempura, in one key respect: to cook tempura, you dip ingredients in a light batter and deep-fry. With kara-age, on the other hand, you simply dredge seasoned ingredients in flour or potato starch before tossing into a vat of bubbling oil. (Granted, you don't exactly need a vat.)

So, yes, kara-age is easy to cook, especially compared to the more challenging tempura. But that doesn't mean this dish isn't taken seriously. In fact, in Japan there even exists a group called the Kara-Age Association, which qualifies and licenses chefs for deep-frying duty at restaurants.

That's kind of cool, but you definitely don't need a license to prepare this style of dish at home. Kara-age is a home cooking standard in Japan, enjoyed in every corner of the country (more common at home than tempura). It's so delicious to enjoy, and even fantastic served at room temperature at parties or picnics (the perfect finger food). Kara-age is also a must for bento box lunches, and it even finds its way between slices of bread to make a tasty sandwich.

TATSUTA-AGE

It's a delightfully poetic name—Tatsuta is the name of a river famous for the russet-colored leaves floating downstream in autumn, leaves that evoke the color of fried chicken, evoking super flavorful, beautifully crunchy bird. Tatsuta-age is truly fried chicken perfection, but as you'll see in the recipe that follows, it's also a snap to prepare. So what gives? In a word, marinating. You marinate the chicken in umami-bomb Japanese seasonings (sake, soy sauce, mirin) and aromatic garlic and ginger before coating in potato starch, which envelopes the chicken in such a delightfully light, crunchy crust. Simple. But not that simple. As Tadashi likes to say, only half-jokingly, in Japanese cuisine the producers do most of the work: in this case, we tip our hats to the brewers who infused those seasonings with such amazing, deep flavor. And because it's marinated, you don't need to use any sauces or dipping sauces; this chicken stands triumphantly on its own. Tatsuta-age is usually cooked with dark meat chicken (tastier), with the skin on (tastier), and boneless (hey, chopstick culture). But if you want to use skinless white meat, we won't protest. Finally, if you want to add another flavor pop, deep-fry the chicken in part or all toasted sesame oil, which is fantastic.

SERVES 4

4 chicken legs (about 2 pounds), boned and cut into 2-inch pieces

2 cloves garlic, peeled and grated

1/2 teaspoon salt

4 teaspoons grated ginger

1/4 cup sake

1/4 cup soy sauce

2 tablespoons mirin

1 cup katakuriko (potato starch)

Vegetable oil for deep-frying

Steamed rice, for serving

1 lemon, cut into wedges (optional)

Mix together the chicken, garlic, salt, ginger, sake, soy sauce, and mirin in a bowl until well combined. Marinate the chicken for 15 minutes.

In another bowl add the *katakuriko*. When the chicken is ready, squeeze excess marinade from the chicken with your hands and dredge each piece in the *katakuriko*. Shake off the excess starch. Place the dredged chicken pieces on a plate. (Alternatively, pour the *katakuriko* into a zip-top storage bag, add pieces of the chicken, seal the bag, and shake until the chicken is coated with the starch. Repeat

until all the chicken is coated. Place the dredged chicken pieces on a plate.)

Place a cast-iron skillet on a burner. Fill the skillet with vegetable oil to a height of at least 1 inch. Attach a deep-fry (or "candy") thermometer to the side of the skillet. On a work surface near the skillet, set up a tray lined with newspaper or paper towels to drain the cooked tatsuta age. Turn the heat on to high. Heat the oil to 340°F.

When the oil has heated to 340°F, add the chicken to the skillet. Depending on the size of the skillet, cook the chicken in

continued >

Kara-age

batches. Be careful not to overfill the skillet, which will lower the cooking temperature; use, at most, half of the surface area of the oil to cook. While the chicken is frying, check the oil temperature with a candy thermometer. Regulate the heat to maintain a constant 340°F oil temperature. If the oil is too hot, the chicken will burn; if too low, the chicken will come out soggy and greasy.

Fry the chicken for about 5 minutes, until the chicken turns golden brown. When it's ready, transfer the chicken to the paper-lined plate to drain. Serve piping hot with steamed white rice and the lemon wedges on the side. Squeeze lemon juice on the chicken, to taste.

IKA-AGE

Now we introduce deep-fried squid, Japanese style. Much like tatsuta-age, the squid (*ika* in Japanese) in this recipe is marinated, dusted in flour in this case, and deep-fried. Unlike run-of-the-mill calamari, which is batter coated and oily and needs to dip in something, our squid is lighter and crunchier and requires no sauce. In this recipe Tadashi also adds *yuzu kosho* (see page 236) for a hint of citrusy, fiery heat, a contemporary touch that works so beautifully with the squid. Keep in mind that the squid deep-fries quickly, in about a minute, so be careful not to burn.

SERVES 4

2 tablespoons red yuzu kosho (see page 236)

¼ cup soy sauce

¼ cup sake

1 teaspoon grated ginger

1 pound squid, cleaned and sliced into ½-inch-thick pieces

Vegetable oil for deep-frying

1 cup flour

1 tablespoon thinly sliced scallion

Mix together the *yuzu kosho*, soy sauce, sake, and ginger in a bowl. Add the squid and mix together with your hands for about 30 seconds, until all the squid pieces are well combined. Let the squid marinate at room temperature for 15 minutes.

While the squid is marinating, place a cast-iron skillet on a burner. Fill the skillet with vegetable oil to a height of at least 1 inch. Attach a deep-fry (or "candy") thermometer to the side of the skillet. On a work surface near the skillet, set up a tray lined with newspaper or paper towels to drain the cooked squid.

When the squid is ready, turn the heat under the oil on to high. Heat the oil to 350°F.

Add the flour to another mixing bowl. Squeeze the excess liquid from the squid with your hands, and drop the squid pieces into the flour. Use your hands to toss the squid so each piece is evenly coated with the flour.

When the oil has heated to 350°F, shake off the excess flour from the squid and carefully add them to the oil. Depending on the size of the skillet, cook the squid in batches. Be careful not to overfill the skillet, which will lower the cooking temperature; use, at most, half of the surface area of the oil to cook.

Cook the squid for about 1 minute, until they turn golden brown. When they're ready, use a spider or similar implement to transfer the squid to the paper-lined plate to drain. When all the squid have been cooked and drained, transfer to a serving platter and garnish with the scallions. Serve immediately.

Kara-age

NAGOYA TEBASAKI

SERVES 4

Nagoya, in central Japan, is a city that's nuts about chicken. Its citizens grill it, poach it, even eat it raw. A half century or so ago, the chef of a local joint called Furaibo noticed mountains of chicken wings at the local market going begging for customers. Why waste wings, he pondered. So he came up with a recipe and started offering these forlorn parts at Furaibo. The result was, well, spectacular. In short order, those mountains at the market turned into barren valleys as shoppers, and other restaurants, began snapping up the wings in Nagoya, and beyond. The secret to these amazing wings is to deep-fry the chicken first, then quickly dip them into a marinade for flavor. Here's Tadashi's delicious variation. Be sure to bring some extra napkins to the dining table.

16 chicken wings (about 2 pounds)

Salt

Pepper

1 teaspoon tobanjan (see page 236)

2 teaspoons grated garlic

2 tablespoons sugar

2 tablespoons red miso (see page 235)

2 tablespoons soy sauce

¼ cup sake

¼ cup mirin

Vegetable oil for deep-frying

¼ cup katakuriko (potato starch)

1 tablespoon sesame seed

Cut each chicken wing at its 2 joints, resulting in 3 parts for each wing. Discard the "wingtip" part of the wings (that is, the *entire* third part, which will burn when deep-frying). Lightly season the chicken with salt and pepper. Transfer to a large bowl and set aside.

Add the *tobanjan*, garlic, sugar, miso, soy sauce, sake, and mirin to a saucepan and place over high heat. Cook, stirring constantly, until the sugar and miso dissolve and the sauce comes to a boil. Transfer the sauce to a large mixing bowl and set aside.

Place a cast-iron skillet on a burner. Fill the skillet with vegetable oil to a height of at least 1 inch. Attach a deep-fry (or "candy") thermometer to the side of the skillet. On a work surface near the skillet, set up a tray lined with newspaper or paper towels to drain the cooked wings. Turn the heat on to high. Heat the oil to 350°F.

While the oil is heating, add the *katakuriko* to the bowl with the chicken wings and toss until all the wings are evenly coated.

When the oil has heated to 350°F, shake off the excess *katakuriko* from the wings and carefully lay them in the oil. Depending on the size of the skillet, cook the wings in batches. Be careful not to overfill the skillet, which will lower the cooking temperature; use, at most, half of the surface area of the oil to cook. While the wings are cooking, check the oil temperature with a candy thermometer. Regulate the heat to maintain a constant 350°F oil temperature.

Cook the wings for about 7 minutes, until they are cooked through and turn golden. The wings will float to the surface when they're done. When they're ready, transfer the wings to the paper-lined plate to drain. When all the wings have been cooked, add them to the bowl with the sauce. Toss for about 1 minute, until the wings are evenly coated with the sauce. Transfer the wings to a serving platter, garnish with the sesame seed, and serve immediately.

SESAME CHICKEN

SERVES 4

Instead of flour or potato starch, here we coat marinated chicken with sesame seeds. When deep-fried, the chicken comes out tender and juicy, but it's the sesame seeds—browned, nutty, and incredibly fragrant—that put this dish over the top. Use raw sesame seeds if you can find them.

1 pound boneless chicken breast, cut into 1-inch cubes

½ teaspoon salt

4 teaspoons grated ginger

¼ cup sake

¼ cup soy sauce

2 tablespoons mirin

½ cup sesame seed (preferably raw, but you can use toasted sesame seed, too)

Vegetable oil for deep-frying

Steamed rice, for serving

Mix together the chicken, salt, ginger, sake, soy sauce, and mirin in a bowl until well combined. Marinate the chicken for 15 minutes.

In another bowl, add the sesame seed. When the chicken is ready, squeeze excess marinade from the chicken with your hands and dredge each piece in the sesame seed, coating both sides well. Place the coated chicken pieces on a plate.

Place a cast-iron skillet on a burner. Fill the skillet with vegetable oil to a height of at least 1 inch. Attach a deep-fry (or "candy") thermometer to the side of the skillet. On a work surface near the skillet, set up a tray lined with newspaper or paper towels to drain the cooked sesame chicken. Turn the heat on to high. Heat the oil to 340°F.

When the oil has heated to 340°F, add the chicken to the skillet. Depending on the size of the skillet, cook the chicken in batches. Be careful not to overfill the skillet, which will lower the cooking temperature; use, at most, half of the surface area of the oil to cook. While the chicken is frying, check the oil temperature with a candy thermometer. Regulate the heat to maintain a constant 340°F oil temperature. If the oil is too hot, the chicken will burn; if too low, the chicken will come out soggy and greasy.

Fry the chicken for about 4 minutes, until the chicken turns golden brown. Be careful that the sesame seed doesn't burn. When it's ready, transfer the chicken to the paper-lined plate to drain. Serve piping hot with steamed white rice on the side.

Kara-age

FISH KARA-AGE

There's something so elemental about gathering friends and family around a beautifully fried whole fish and going at it with chopsticks. We use sea bass, but you can also cook this dish with red snapper, flounder, striped bass, or a small grouper. The trick is making cuts into the fish's body beforehand so you can easily pick the flesh off with said chopsticks (see page 104 for how-to photos). You want to cut on an angle, which helps heat move through the flesh so the fish cooks more evenly. *Momiji oroshi* is a condiment traditionally made from daikon grated with whole dried chilies. Here we make a fast version with grated daikon and red *yuzu kosho* (see page 236); when added to the ponzu sauce, it lends a fiery flavor and thickens the sauce to help it adhere to bites of fish.

4 whole sea bass (about 4 pounds total), scaled, gutted, and cleaned (leave the head on)

Salt

Shichimi togarashi (see page 235)

¼ cup grated daikon (extra liquid squeezed off)

½ teaspoon red yuzu kosho (see page 236)

Vegetable oil for deep-frying

1 cup katakuriko (potato starch)

4 tablespoons sliced scallion

2 cups ponzu (page 105), poured into 4 small bowls

2 lemons, cut into wedges

To prepare the fish, make 4 horizontal cuts along the fish, from the head to the tail. Cut to the spine. Now cut diagonal notches from the top fin to the belly, about 1 inch apart along the length of the fish. Cut on an angle, to the bone. See "How to Prepare a Whole Fish for Deep-Frying" (page 104) for step-by-step instructions with photographs. Repeat on the other side of the fish. Season the fish on both sides with the salt and *shichimi togarashi*, making sure to season the flesh inside the cuts. Repeat with the remaining fish.

To prepare "fast" *momiji oroshi*, mix together the grated daikon with the red *yuzu kosho* in a small bowl and set aside.

Place a large cast-iron skillet on a burner. Fill the skillet with vegetable oil to a height of at least 2 inches. Attach a deep-fry (or "candy") thermometer to the side of the skillet. On a work surface near the skillet, set up a tray lined with newspaper or paper towels to drain the cooked fish. Turn the heat on to high. Heat the oil to 350°F.

While the oil is heating, pour the *katakuriko* onto a large plate or tray. Dredge the fish on both sides, making sure the *katakuriko* coats the inside of the cuts. Shake off the excess. Transfer the coated fish to a clean plate and repeat with the remaining fish.

Deep-fry the fish one at a time. When the oil has heated to 350°F, carefully lay the fish into the oil. While the fish is cooking, check the oil temperature with a candy thermometer. Regulate the heat to maintain a constant 350°F oil temperature.

Cook for about 5 minutes, turning once, until the fish begins to float in the oil. Transfer the fish to the paper-lined tray to drain. Repeat with the remaining fish.

Serve each fish on a plate with 1 tablespoon mound of the *momiji oroshi*, 1 tablespoon of scallions, and one-fourth of the lemon wedges, with the ponzu on the side. To eat, squeeze the lemon over the fish. Add a little *momiji oroshi* and scallions to the ponzu. Dip bites of the fish into the ponzu.

How to Prepare a Whole Fish for Deep-Frying

1 Lay the fish flat on a cutting board

2 Cut along the spine from head to tail

3 Cut along the belly from head to tail

4 Make two more cuts along the center of the fish

5 Cut diagonal notches from the top fin to the belly

6 The cuts should be on an angle and reach to the bone

7 The fish is ready for deep-frying

Ponzu

Ponzu is a citrusy, vinegary dipping sauce that's a fundamental flavoring agent in Japanese cooking. You can buy it ready made, but nothing on those store shelves beats making it yourself. Use a combination of citrus juices, bottled yuzu juice, or just lemon juice, which works fine, too. Ponzu will keep in the refrigerator for up to two weeks.

3 tablespoons sake

1 tablespoon mirin

½ cup soy sauce

¼ cup citrus juice (any combination of lemon, lime, grapefruit, and orange juice—preferably at least half lemon juice)

¼ cup rice vinegar

¼ cup water

1 (6-inch) piece kombu

¼ cup (about ⅛ ounce) tightly packed dried, shaved bonito flakes (katsuobushi)

Add the sake and mirin to a small saucepan and bring to a boil over high heat. Boil for 1 minute, remove from the heat, and let the liquid come to room temperature.

In a bowl, stir together the soy sauce, citrus juice, vinegar, water, sake mixture, kombu, and bonito flakes. Cover loosely with plastic wrap and let the mixture steep in the refrigerator for 12 hours, or overnight. Strain the ponzu through a cheesecloth or fine sieve; gently squeeze to press out the liquid.

7 TEMPURA

TEMPURA

We figure tempura runs second only to sushi in the iconic Japanese foods department, and for good reason: no other style of deep-frying can produce such a light, airy, crunchy crust that, remarkably, doesn't taste greasy, and at the same time accentuates the natural flavors and textures of the cooked ingredients. Tempura is often elevated to a high art in Japan, where chefs at specialized *tempura-ya* ("tempura shops") serve their sublime fried morsels in rounds as soon as they're ready, but this cooking has humbler roots and remains a mainstay of casual eateries, soba shops, and home kitchens—our kind of tempura.

For such a signature Japanese dish, you'll be surprised to know that tempura traces back to deep-frying introduced by Portuguese traders in the 1600s. It was adapted and evolved by Japanese, and before long it became a mainstay of humble vegetarian cooking of Buddhist temples as well as popular street food in old Edo (the former name of Tokyo), sold by pushcart vendors plying the packed streets. Today the pushcarts are gone, but tempura is still sold to go from tiny storefronts across the country, a tasty meal to share with family and friends.

Tempura is typically prepared with vegetables and seafood. Meat and poultry are not usually cooked this way—too heavy—but we have heard of ice cream, chocolate, even gummy bear tempura (yuk). What's truly amazing about tempura is that, at its core, we're talking about dipping ingredients into a simple batter of flour, water, and egg yolk, and deep-frying in vegetable oil—that's it. But of course, *how* you dip the ingredients, *how* you mix the batter, and *how* you deep-fry make all the difference between sublime and, well, not so great.

But don't worry. In the chapter that follows, we'll walk you through everything you need to know about tempura making, step by step, with plenty of how-to photos to guide you. We break down the recipes that follow by ingredients to help you understand how to specifically cook them. A classic tempura meal includes shrimp and vegetables, and sometimes other seafood—you want a variety of flavors and textures. So plan to cook a bunch of different foods tempura style—that's the fun of it!

Tempura is traditionally served with one of two accompaniments: a light, soy sauce–infused dipping sauce mixed with grated daikon and ginger (ten tsuyu, page 111) or sea salt (or sea salt mixed with *matcha*, powdered green tea). You can eat tempura as a side dish or the main event, for lunch or dinner, or even for breakfast with hot soba.

Remember, with a little practice, you'll soon be biting into a beautiful piece of tempura, with its irresistible nutty aroma wafting your way. And then you'll know: yeah, baby, I got the technique down!

TEMPURA BATTER

Master Recipe

This is the most critical step to making tempura. Get the batter right, and your tempura will have a light, lacy, sublime crust with incredible crispiness. Get it wrong, and you're venturing into corn-dog territory—your tempura will come out with a thick, bready crust, not what you want. How to cook it corn-dog free? First, wait until the oil is heating, the last step before cooking, to combine the dry and wet parts of the batter. Use four chopsticks held together, as we explain below, to mix the batter. This bunch of chopsticks is a much less efficient mixer than a spoon or spatula, which is exactly the point. And finally, as we caution below—don't overmix. To understand why, check out "How to Make Tempura Batter" (page 110).

2 egg yolks

2 cups cold water

¼ cup ice cubes

2 cups cake flour

Combine the yolks and water in a bowl, mixing until they're incorporated, then add the ice cubes (the "wet" part of the batter). In another bowl or container, add the flour (the "dry" part of the batter).

When you're ready to cook the tempura, quickly add the flour to the liquid, in one shot. Hold 4 chopsticks together, the tips pointed down, like you're grabbing a bottle. Stab at the batter with the chopsticks, mashing down again and again to combine the dry and wet parts. Do not stir; you barely want to mix the batter. Mix for about 30 seconds, or until the batter becomes loose and liquidy, with the consistency of heavy cream. It should be lumpy, with visible gobs of dry flour floating in the liquid, and with unmixed flour sticking to the sides of the bowl. Remember, if you overmix the batter, you'll ruin it.

The Secret to Great Tempura

The three most important things to keep in mind when making tempura:

1. The batter is the most critical step to tempura—prepare it just before deep-frying.
2. Oil temperature is key—it has to be exactly right or the tempura will come out soggy or burned.
3. Be systematic about making tempura—set up your fry station ahead of time so you can work quickly and efficiently.

Tempura

How to Make Tempura Batter

Let's geek out for a minute and consider how tempura batter actually works.

Tempura batter seems simple enough—just flour, egg yolks, and water. But how these humble elements transform into that amazing airy, crispy crust is nothing short of miraculous. The key is controlling the glutens in the flour. Glutens are created by the flour's proteins; they're what give dough elasticity and bread its chewiness. With tempura, the goal is to minimize gluten formation. That's why we use cake flour, with the lowest amount of protein of any flour. And that's why we barely mix the batter with the clunky bunch o' chopsticks, so the glutens in the flour don't become activated. Furthermore, that's why we mix the dry and wet parts of the batter at the last minute, so the glutens don't have time to relax. So tempura batter never has a chance to get bready and stretchy.

Also, because we mix the batter in the last minute, the flour particles don't have time to absorb much moisture, so when a battered ingredient hits the hot oil, that small amount of moisture quickly evaporates, further increasing the tempura's crispiness.

The batter is kept cold with the ice cubes to make it more viscous, which helps it adhere to foods (dredging in flour helps with this, too). The lumpy, uneven consistency of the batter, with its gobs of unmixed flour, helps create tempura's signature lacy crust. Finally, that crispy batter creates a barrier between ingredients and the oil they're frying in, which is why tempura done right doesn't taste greasy and retains natural flavors and textures so magnificently.

1 Use a handful of chopsticks to mix the yolks and water

2 Add ice cubes to the egg mixture

3 Add the flour

4 Stab at the batter to combine until it has the consistency of heavy cream—don't overmix!

TEMPURA DIPPING SAUCE (TEN TSUYU)

Master Recipe

Here is the recipe for ten tsuyu, the classic dipping sauce that accompanies tempura. You'll see that the ratio of dashi to soy sauce to mirin is 4:1:1, so if you want to make more or less dipping sauce, just follow this proportion. The sauce is served with grated daikon and ginger on the side, which you add to the liquid before dunking in a piece of tempura. Besides adding fresh flavor, the grated ingredients give body to the sauce, making it easier to adhere to the tempura.

4 SERVINGS

1 cup dashi (page 161)

¼ cup soy sauce

¼ cup mirin

8 ounces daikon, peeled thickly, so you can see the radish's translucent flesh

½-inch piece ginger (about 1 ounce), peeled

Combine the dashi, soy sauce, and mirin in a small saucepan. Place over medium heat. As soon as the dipping sauce comes to a boil, turn off the heat. When you're ready to serve, reheat over low heat.

Grate the daikon on the coarsest side of a box grater. Squeeze out excess liquid and set aside. Grate the ginger finely. Serve the grated daikon and ginger on the side of the dipping sauce. When you're ready to eat, add the daikon and ginger to the dipping sauce and dip the tempura into it.

Tempura

VEGETABLE TEMPURA

Use any combination of vegetables for tempura, including lotus root, broccoli, kabocha squash, pumpkin, eggplant, sweet potato, shiitake and any other mushrooms, carrot, zucchini, okra, broccoli, peppers, and asparagus—the list is as long as the vegetables available at your market. You can also use tender leaves like shiso, a delicacy in Japan. With leaves, batter only one side and fry quickly for about 30 seconds.

SERVES 4

1 recipe tempura batter (page 109)

1 pound vegetables, sliced on an angle into bite-size pieces

½ cup cake flour

2 quarts vegetable oil

¼ cup toasted sesame oil

Tempura dipping sauce (page 111)

Prepare the wet and dry parts of the batter, following the master recipe (page 109).

To prepare a tempura cooking station, beside your burner, arrange the vegetables, a plate with the cake flour, and the wet and dry parts of the batter. Also, ready a tray lined with paper towels or newspaper to absorb the excess oil from the cooked vegetables, and the tools you'll need: chopsticks, a metal strainer, and a candy thermometer, if you have one. Place a cooking vessel on the burner; use one with a uniform size to heat oil evenly, like a large cast-iron skillet or Dutch oven (don't use a wok). Add the vegetable oil and sesame oil.

Heat the oil to 360°F over high heat. Use a candy thermometer or follow the old-school method to judge the temperature (see page 115).

While the oil is heating, prepare the tempura batter, following the master method (page 110).

When the oil has reached 360°F, prepare to cook the vegetables in batches. See "How to Cook Tempura" (page 114) for step-by-step instructions and photographs. Be careful not to overfill the skillet, which will lower the cooking temperature; use, at most, half of the surface area of the oil to cook. While the tempura is cooking, check the oil temperature with a candy thermometer. Regulate the heat to maintain a constant 360°F oil temperature. If the oil is too hot, the tempura will burn; if too low, the tempura will come out soggy and greasy.

Lightly dredge the vegetables in the flour, then dip into the batter. Immediately lay the vegetables in the hot oil. Working in batches, deep-fry the harder vegetables like sweet potato, carrot, or lotus root first, for about 3 minutes, until the vegetables turn golden brown. Transfer the vegetables to the prepared tray to drain excess oil. Repeat with the other vegetables. Cook softer vegetables like asparagus, broccoli, and pumpkin for about 2 minutes. For shiso leaves, dredge only one side of the leaf with flour, and cook for about 1 minute.

Serve the vegetable tempura with the dipping sauce on the side.

How to Cook Tempura

1 Add a touch of sesame oil to the pan

2 Dredge the shrimp in flour

3 Dip into the batter just before frying

4 Fry the tempura

5 Place on the prepared tray

Judging Temperature the Old-School Way

Oil temperature is so important to this cooking that we urge you to buy a good-quality deep-fry (or "candy") thermometer and use it when frying. But once you get the hang of making tempura, you can also judge oil temperature the old-school way—by dripping a couple of drops of tempura batter into the hot oil. If the batter sinks all the way to the bottom of your pot and then pops up to the surface, the oil temperature is about 330°F. If the batter sinks only to the middle of the oil, then pops to the surface, the oil temperature is about 350°F. If the batter just sizzles on the surface when it hits the oil, then the temperature is 360°F and higher. So you want to add tempura to the oil just after the drops sink to the middle and pop up (when it's about to hit 360°F).

How to Prepare Shrimp for Tempura

1 Peel the shrimp

2 Make a shallow cut along the back and devein the shrimp

3 Cut notches into the back of the shrimp

4 Flatten the shrimp with your fingers

SHRIMP TEMPURA

Shrimp is the *sine qua non* of tempura cooking. A beautiful, golden, crispy shrimp—straight and long and fragrant—is pure tempura joy. The cutting technique we explain in the recipe is how you keep the shrimp from curling when it hits the hot oil (straight shrimp is a classic Japanese aesthetic touch). You'll also see we drip more tempura batter onto the shrimp as they cook. This is a technique called *hana sakasu*, which makes the shrimp even more crispy and crusty. When you drip this batter, bits will break off and start frying on their own. Skim and save the bits, called tenkasu, and use them to make tendon (page 149). (You can freeze the tenkasu to save for later.)

SERVES 4

8 large shrimp (16/20 size, about 8 ounces)
1 recipe tempura batter (page 109)
1/2 cup cake flour
2 quarts vegetable oil
1/4 cup toasted sesame oil
Tempura dipping sauce (page 111)

Peel the shrimp but leave the last joint of the shell intact. (See opposite for step-by-step photographs.) Devein from the back, then turn the shrimp over. Cut 4 or 5 notches 1/4 inch deep into the flesh, and trim the tail by a sliver (this allows moisture inside the tail to escape). Using your thumb and index finger, gently pinch the shrimp to flatten and straighten it; be careful not to break the soft flesh. Repeat for all the shrimp. Allow the shrimp to dry (blot with paper towels if needed) and come to room temperature.

Prepare the wet and dry parts of the batter, following the master method (page 109).

To prepare a tempura cooking station, beside your burner, arrange the shrimp, a plate with the cake flour, and the wet and dry parts of the batter. Also, ready a tray lined with paper towels or newspaper to absorb the excess oil from the cooked shrimp, and the tools you'll need: chopsticks, a metal strainer, and a candy

thermometer, if you have one. Place a cooking vessel on the burner; use one with a uniform size to heat oil evenly, like a large cast-iron skillet or Dutch oven (don't use a wok). Add the vegetable oil and sesame oil.

Heat the oil to 360°F over high heat. Use a candy thermometer or follow the old-school method to judge the temperature (see page 115).

While the oil is heating, combine the wet and dry parts of the tempura batter, following the master recipe (page 109).

When the oil has reached 360°F, prepare to cook the shrimp in batches. (See "How to Cook Tempura" (page 114) for step-by-step instructions and photographs. Be careful not to overfill the skillet, which will lower the cooking temperature; use, at most, half of the surface area of the oil to cook. While the tempura is cooking, check the oil temperature with a candy

continued >

thermometer. Regulate the heat to maintain a constant 360°F oil temperature. If the oil is too hot, the tempura will burn; if too low, the tempura will come out soggy and greasy.

Lightly dredge the shrimp in the flour, then dip it into the batter. Immediately ease the shrimp into the hot oil. Separate and stretch out the shrimp with chopsticks. While they cook, use the ends of your fingers to drip more batter on top of the shrimp. Skim the oil with the skimmer to remove any excess bits of batter and keep the oil clean. Cook for about

3 minutes, until the shrimp turn golden brown, and the bubbles around the shrimp have grown larger and are bubbling less intensely and not as loudly as when the shrimp was first added to the oil. Transfer the shrimp to the prepared tray. Use a deep tray, if possible, and lean the shrimp against its sides to stand them up to drain excess oil (but if you don't have a deep tray, don't worry). Repeat with the remaining shrimp.

Serve the shrimp tempura with the dipping sauce on the side.

LEMON SOLE TEMPURA

Fish tempura is typically prepared with white-fleshed fish. Here we use lemon sole, but flounder, cod, scrod, sea bass, snapper, and tiny smelt (called *kisu* in Japan) also make amazing tempura. And don't forget scallops, sea eel, and squid—cook them the same way we describe below.

SERVES 4

4 fillets lemon sole (about 1 pound), cut in half lengthwise through the centerline

1 recipe tempura batter (page 109)

$1/2$ cup cake flour

Vegetable oil, for frying

$1/4$ cup toasted sesame oil

Tempura dipping sauce (page 111)

For each lemon sole fillet, make parallel cuts on the skin side, about $1/8$ inch apart. This will keep the fish from curling when it deep-fries.

Prepare the wet and dry parts of the batter, following the master method (page 110).

To prepare a tempura cooking station, beside your burner, arrange the fish, a plate with the cake flour, and the wet and dry parts of the batter. Also, ready a tray lined with paper towels or newspaper to absorb the excess oil from the cooked fish, and the tools you'll need: chopsticks, a metal strainer, and a candy thermometer, if you have one. Place a cooking vessel on the burner; use one with a uniform size to heat oil evenly, like a large cast-iron skillet or Dutch oven (don't use a wok). Add the vegetable oil and sesame oil to a height of 1 inch (you want the oil shallow for this tempura).

Heat the oil to 360°F over high heat. Use a candy thermometer or follow the old-school method to judge the temperature (see page 115).

While the oil is heating, combine the wet and dry parts of the tempura batter, following the master recipe (page 109).

When the oil has reached 360°F, prepare to cook the fish in batches. See "How to Cook Tempura" (page 114) for step-by-step instructions and photographs. Be careful not to overfill the skillet, which will lower the cooking temperature; use, at most, half of the surface area of the oil to cook. While the tempura is cooking, check the oil temperature with a candy thermometer. Regulate the heat to maintain a constant 360°F oil temperature. If the oil is too hot, the tempura will burn; if too low, the tempura will come out soggy and greasy.

Lightly dredge the fish in the flour, then dip it into the batter. Immediately lay the fish in the hot oil. Cook for about 3 minutes, until the fish turns golden brown. Transfer the fish to the prepared tray to drain excess oil. Repeat with the remaining fish.

Serve the fish tempura with the dipping sauce on the side.

SHRIMP-SHIITAKE KAKI-AGE

Kaki-age ("kaki-ageh") are tempura fritters, the most down-to-earth—and forgiving—style of tempura cooking. While classic tempura can be elevated to an art form, kaki-age is always considered comforting, home-style cooking. Kaki-age with hot soba or udon is amazing; in fact, stand-up noodle joints at many a train station in Japan serve nothing but. And don't forget kaki-age over a steaming bowl of rice, with the kaki-age first dipped into tempura dipping sauce (page 111)—so good. Kaki-age can also be eaten at room temperature, so it's perfect for bento box lunches. And finally, you can freeze kaki-age, so make a bunch for later. (The kaki-age won't be crispy when it defrosts, but floating over soba or udon, or dipped in sauce and served on top of rice, it will still be incredibly tasty.) Here we make kaki-age with shrimp and shiitake, followed by three delicious variations. Once you get the feel of it, try making kaki-age with other vegetables and seafood; these tempura fritters are easy and foolproof. Do not use ice when preparing the batter (unlike classic tempura); the ice can explode when hitting the hot oil if it's accidentally added to the fritter. We cook the tempura for three minutes on the first side, then flip and cook one minute more because the batter sinks when it hits the oil, so the bottom needs more time to cook through.

SERVES 4 (MAKES 4 KAKI-AGE)

tempura batter

2 egg yolks

2 cups cold water

2 cups cake flour

8 ounces small peeled shrimp (51/60 size)

2 quarts vegetable oil

¼ cup toasted sesame oil

1 cup thinly sliced shiitake (about 4 shiitake, stemmed)

1 cup sliced scallions (about 3 scallions, cleaned and trimmed), cut on an angle into 1-inch pieces

12 shiso leaves, thinly sliced

1 tablespoon flour

Tempura dipping sauce (page 111)

To make the kaki-age batter, combine the egg yolks and water in a bowl, mixing until they're incorporated. In another bowl or container, add the flour (the "dry" part of the batter).

To prepare a tempura cooking station, beside your burner, arrange the shrimp and the wet and dry parts of the batter. Also, ready a tray lined with paper towels or newspaper to absorb the excess oil from the cooked shrimp, and the tools you'll need: chopsticks, a metal strainer, and a candy thermometer, if you have one. Place a cooking vessel on the burner; use one with a uniform size to heat oil evenly, like a large cast-iron skillet or Dutch oven (don't use a wok). Add the vegetable oil and sesame oil.

continued >

Add the shrimp, shiitake, scallions, shiso, and flour to a bowl and gently mix together, until all the ingredients are coated with the flour.

Heat the oil to 350°F over high heat. Use a candy thermometer or follow the old-school method to judge the temperature (see page 115).

While the oil is heating, combine the wet and dry parts of the tempura batter, following the master method (page 109). Add the batter to the shrimp mixture and gently mix together.

When the oil has reached 350°F, prepare to cook the kaki-age in batches. See "How to Cook Tempura" (page 114) for step-by-step instructions and photographs. Scoop about one-fourth of the ingredients with

your hands and pack it together to form into a patty. Gently ease the patty into the center of the oil. While the kaki-age is cooking, check the oil temperature with a candy thermometer. Regulate the heat to maintain a constant 350°F oil tempera-ture. If the oil is too hot, the kaki-age will burn; if too low, the kaki-age will come out soggy and greasy.

Cook for about 3 minutes, then turn the kaki-age. Cook for 1 minute more, until the kaki-age turns golden brown. Transfer to the prepared tray; stand the kaki-age up if possible to drain excess oil. Repeat to make the remaining kaki-age.

Cut each kaki-age into 4 pieces. Stack on a plate, and serve immediately with the dip-ping sauce on the side.

KAKI-AGE VARIATIONS

Follow the Shrimp-Shiitake Kaki-Age recipe (page 121) but for the shrimp, shiitake, scallions, shiso, and flour substitute with the ingredients listed below.

Onion Kaki-Age

1 pound onions, peeled
1 tablespoon cake flour

Cut the onions in half lengthwise, from top to bottom (axis to axis). Cut each half into 1/4-inch slices, also cutting lengthwise.

Separate the pieces and mix together with the flour in a bowl. Follow the recipe instructions on page 121.

Burdock-Carrot Kaki-Age

8 ounces burdock, cleaned and julienned
1 small carrot (about 2 ounces), peeled and julienned
1 tablespoon cake flour

Combine the burdock, carrot, and flour in a bowl and mix together well. Follow the recipe instructions on page 121.

Asparagus Kaki-Age

¾ pound asparagus
1 tablespoon cake flour

Trim the asparagus and peel the bottom 2 inches of the stalk if woody. Thinly slice the asparagus on an angle into pieces about 1 inch long.

Combine the asparagus and flour in a bowl and mix together. Follow the recipe instructions on page 121.

8 OKONOMIYAKI

OKONOMIYAKI

Let's turn our attention now to pancakes. But forget buttermilk, sliced bananas, and maple syrup, because in Japan the pancakes are a whole different flapjack—savory, hearty, and oh so good, griddled with everything from cabbage, pork, and ramen noodles to fried eggs and "dancing" dried, shaved bonito. We'll get to the dancing bit in a minute, but first let's talk about "everything." These pancakes are called *okonmiyaki*, which means, essentially, "what you like, cooked." So depending where you eat them, all kinds of stuff are piled on top. The cities and towns on the western side of Japan, like Osaka and Hiroshima, are the okonomiyaki heartland. Each place has its own custom okonomiyaki, with its own favorite toppings. And in each city in the west, you'll find row after row of restaurants featuring long flat-top griddles, with a cook on one side and customers on the other, who are watching, waiting, and ultimately going to town on freshly made pancakes.

Okonomiyaki are thought to have derived from pancakes in the Tokyo area, and a crepe in Kyoto known as "one-penny Western food." ("Western" in this case meaning European.) The common thread here is that price tag. Okonomiyaki is frugal eating; in its early forms, it consisted of mostly cabbage in a flour pancake. (In fact, its popularity expanded across Japan during the difficult days of reconstruction after World War II, when they were often sold from tiny shops run by war widows.)

But inexpensive doesn't mean insignificant. Okonomiyaki wouldn't be okonomiyaki without a bevy of tasty toppings, which add flavor and visual panache. These include Otofuku sauce, a thickened, sweetened Worcestershire sauce, like tonkatsu sauce (page 62); bright green *aonori* powdered seaweed; Kewpie mayonnaise (see page 132); and dried, shaved bonito. Make that "dancing" dried, shaved bonito—when you sprinkle the tissue-thin shavings over the hot pancake they start shimmying like they're dancing the funky chicken, a delightful little feat.

When you taste okonomiyaki, you'll understand why they're so addictive. While they're popular restaurant dishes, these pancakes are also terrific cooked at home—they're the perfect party food. In fact, in Japan many families own electric flat-top griddles just for this dish, but you can easily cook it in a skillet. In the recipes that follow, we share two of the most popular styles, plus a couple of related dishes.

OSAKA-STYLE OKONOMIYAKI

The okonomiyaki of Osaka is the style that defines this dish. Here, ingredients are simply mixed together with batter and griddled. Cabbage is the mainstay, and there's usually pork. We use fresh pork belly, but ground pork is common, too (more old-fashioned, but delicious). In Osaka, you can also find okonomiyaki cooked with octopus, squid, shrimp, sliced chicken, just veggies, scallions, or kimchee. So feel free to mix and match. A few things to keep in mind: while green or savoy cabbage is best for this dish, just be sure to remove the thick veins from the leaves. And don't chop the cabbage too finely; you want about 1/2-inch square pieces (more or less, don't sweat this). It seems like a lot of cabbage at first, but the leaves cook down quickly—and cabbage is what this dish is all about. Cook the okonomiyaki one at a time (make four pancakes). To eat, cut into quarters and use chopsticks.

SERVES 4

2 cups flour

1 cup dashi (page 161) or water, cold or at room temperature

1 teaspoon salt

1 teaspoon baking powder

2 teaspoons sugar

1 pound cabbage, coarsely chopped (about 10 cups)

4 eggs

1/4 cup toasted sesame oil

8 ounces fresh pork belly, thinly sliced

toppings

Okonomiyaki sauce (see page 234)

Kewpie mayonnaise (see page 132) or other mayonnaise

Aonori (powdered nori seaweed)

Dried, shaved bonito (katsuobushi)

To make the batter, mix together the flour, dashi, salt, baking powder, and sugar in a large bowl. Add the cabbage to the batter and mix well for at least 30 seconds, until all the cabbage is coated. Add the eggs and mix, lightly this time, for about 15 seconds, or until the eggs are just combined with the cabbage.

Preheat a nonstick or cast-iron skillet for at least 5 minutes on medium-low heat. Add 1 tablespoon of the sesame oil, making sure to coat the entire surface of the skillet. Cook the okonomiyaki in batches. Spoon the cabbage and batter mixture into the skillet to form a pancake about 6 inches in diameter and about 1 inch thick. Don't push down on the cabbage; you want a fluffy pancake. Gently lay about one-fourth of the pork belly slices on top of the pancake, trying not to overlap.

Cook the pancake for about 3 minutes. Use a long spatula (a fish spatula is ideal) to carefully flip the pancake, so the side with the pork belly is now facing down. Gently press down on the pancake with the spatula (don't push too hard, you don't want batter spilling from the sides). Cook for about 5 more minutes, then flip the pancake again, so the side with the pork belly is now facing up. (If the okonomiyaki comes apart when you flip it, don't worry; use a spatula to tuck any stray ingredients back into the pancake.) Cook for about 2 more minutes. When it's ready, the pancake should be lightly browned on both sides, the pork cooked through, and the cabbage inside tender.

continued >

Okonomiyaki

Transfer the pancake to a plate, pork side up, and add the toppings. Squeeze about 1 tablespoon of okonomiyaki sauce onto the pancake, in long ribbons. Squeeze about 1 tablespoon of mayonnaise onto the pancake, also in long ribbons. Sprinkle about 1 tablespoon of *aonori* over the pancake. Sprinkle about 1 tablespoon of dried, shaved bonito over the pancake. (Add more or less of any topping, to taste.) Cut the pancake into quarters and serve immediately.

Repeat with the remaining 3 tablespoons oil and pancake batter.

Variation Substitute 8 ounces ground pork for the pork belly. Add the pork to batter after adding the cabbage and mix well. Then add the egg, and mix lightly, to prepare the batter.

Kewpie Mayonnaise

Named after the famous bug-eyed doll, this mayo is Japan's top seller. Compared to American-style mayonnaise (the kind you find in supermarkets), Kewpie is smoother and creamier, has less oil, and is made with a blend of apple and malt vinegars, which bestows an amazing tang that's just addictive. Kewpie also contains a small amount of MSG, which gives it even more kick (one of the few MSG uses we let slide). Sold in a soft bottle so you can squeeze out ribbons of the stuff, it's the go-to mayo for our okonomiyaki recipes—heck, for all the recipes in this book that call for this condiment.

HIROSHIMA-STYLE OKONOMIYAKI

In Hiroshima, about 175 miles west of Osaka as the pigeon flies, the signature okonomiyaki is more of a layered dish that includes a mound of wheat noodles and fried eggs, and a still bigger pile of cabbage, if that's even possible to imagine. It's a bit challenging to cook at home, but it's such an awesome and belly-filling dish that we urge you to give it a try. (Perfect, by the way, for the ravenous football or basketball player in your family.) A large griddle is ideal, but you can get away with two cast-iron skillets. Read the recipe a couple of times to understand the rhythm and how to flip back and forth between the skillets (or sides of the griddle). Also check out the photo series on page 134 for guidance. Cook one pancake at a time, and slather the toppings on artfully.

SERVES 4

1 cup flour

¾ cup dashi (page 161) or water

¼ cup mirin

½ cup plus 4 teaspoons toasted sesame oil

8 ounces cabbage, coarsely chopped (about 5 cups)

4 ounces mung bean sprouts (moyashi) (about 2 cups)

8 ounces fresh pork belly, thinly sliced

¼ cup chopped scallions, white parts only

4 bricks (5 ounces each) yakisoba noodles or fresh-frozen ramen noodles (follow method on page 138)

½ cup water

¼ cup Japanese-style Worchester sauce (see page 234)

4 eggs

¼ cup okonomiyaki sauce (see page 234)

¼ cup aonori (powdered nori seaweed)

Make the batter by whisking together the flour, dashi, and mirin. Set aside.

Place 2 cast-iron skillets on 2 burners, side by side. Preheat the skillets for at least 5 minutes on low heat. Make the okonomiyaki in batches. Add 1 tablespoon of the sesame oil to one skillet, making sure to coat the entire surface of the skillet. Pour batter into the first skillet to form a thin crepe, about 6 inches across. On top of the crepe, pile 2 ounces of cabbage and 1 ounce (1/2 cup) of the sprouts, forming a small mound. Over this mound, lay about 2 ounces of the pork belly strips in rows. Sprinkle 1 tablespoon of chopped scallions on the pork belly. Drip about 1 tablespoon of the batter over the mound, and allow the pancake to cook for about 4 minutes.

While the pancake is cooking, heat 1 tablespoon of sesame oil in the second skillet.

Place 1 brick of yakisoba in the skillet. Use chopsticks to stir-fry the noodles for about 2 minutes. Pour in 2 tablespoons of the water and 1 tablespoon of the Worchester sauce and stir-fry for 1 minute more, and let the noodles simmer.

Return to the first skillet. After 4 minutes, carefully flip the pancake using a long spatula (such as a fish spatula), so the pancake is now on top of the other ingredients. Don't worry if cabbage or other ingredients get a little messy; tuck any stray ingredients back under the pancake. The pancake on top will help the other ingredients steam and cook. Allow the pancake to cook.

Now, go back to the second skillet. Form the noodles into a disk about 6 inches across.

continued >

Okonomiyaki

How to Make
Hiroshima Okonomiyaki

After about 4 more minutes, slide a spatula under the pancake cooking in the first skillet, and carefully transfer it to the second skillet, placing the pancake directly on top of the noodles. They should be roughly the same size.

In the first skillet, now empty, add 1 teaspoon sesame oil and heat for 15 seconds. Crack an egg open and fry it in the skillet, sunny side up. Break the yolk of the egg.

After cooking the pancake and noodles in the second skillet for about 6 minutes, slide a spatula under the pancake and noodles, and carefully transfer to the first skillet, placing directly on top of the frying egg. Remove the second skillet from the heat.

Cook for about 2 minutes, then flip the pancake so now the fried egg is on top. Transfer the pancake to a plate and add the toppings. Squeeze about 1 tablespoon of okonomiyaki sauce onto the pancake, in long ribbons. Sprinkle about 1 tablespoon of *aonori* over the pancake. Cut the pancake into quarters and serve immediately.

Repeat for the remaining 3 pancakes.

**HOW TO MAKE HIROSHIMA
OKONOMIYAKI, opposite:**

1 Pour the batter into the first skillet

2 Form a mound with cabbage and sprouts

3 Layer on pork belly strips in rows

4 Drip batter over the pancake

5 In the second skillet, add the noodles and stir-fry

6 Carefully transfer the pancake from the first skillet to the second

7 Lay the pancake on top of the noodles in the second skillet

8 In the now-empty first skillet, fry an egg

9 Transfer the pancake and noodles on top of the egg in the first skillet

Okonomiyaki

TAKOYAKI

Takoyaki are a fun variation of savory Japanese pancakes, little balls of batter filled with pieces of tasty octopus and griddled. These pillowy morsels are then topped with the usual okonomiyaki toppings and eaten by the mound-full (no, you cannot eat just one). Use toothpicks to spear these suckers and pop them into your mouth. To cook takoyaki, you'll need to use a special metal takoyaki mold (usually nonstick), which are available at Japanese markets. Also, *yamaimo* (also called *nagaimo*) in the ingredients is a type of yam with a slippery, sticky consistency when grated raw that helps add springiness to the takoyaki. You can find *yamaimo* at Japanese markets, but if it's not available, just follow the recipe without it. (The takoyaki will come out a little fluffier than springier, but will still be delicious.)

MAKES ABOUT 28 TAKOYAKI

1½ cups flour

⅓ cup peeled and grated yamaimo (about 2½ ounces)

3 eggs

1¼ cups dashi (page 161)

Toasted sesame oil

4 ounces precooked octopus, cut into about ½ inch cubes

¼ cup chopped scallion

2 tablespoons okonomiyaki sauce (see page 234)

1 tablespoon aonori (powdered nori seaweed)

1 tablespoon dried, shaved bonito

Make the batter by whisking together the flour, *yamaimo*, eggs, and dashi until smooth.

Dip a wad of kitchen towel into the sesame oil and wipe the insides of the takoyaki pan to coat the entire surface, then place the pan over low heat. Preheat for about 2 minutes. When the pan is ready, pour batter into each mold to fill it three-fourths full. To each mold, add about 2 pieces of octopus and a pinch of scallions. Add more batter to each mold until they are full. Make sure not to overflow the molds.

Cook for about 3 minutes. Carefully flip each takoyaki using chopsticks or a skewer. Cook for 3 more minutes. At this point, the takoyaki should be nicely browned all over and feel springy and pillowy.

Use chopsticks or a skewer to transfer the takoyaki to a plate. Squeeze some the okonomiyaki sauce over the takoyaki in ribbons, sprinkle on the *aonori* and dried, shaved bonito, and serve.

YAKISOBA

Yakisoba are Japanese-style fried noodles, so what are they doing in this pancake chapter? Tradition, friend. Okonomiyaki joints customarily offer these noodles as a side to the savory pancakes—both are cooked on a flat-top griddle and use similar seasonings. So who are we to quibble? Yakisoba noodles are like wheat flour ramen noodles but thicker, and they're steamed. (So you're frying cooked noodles.) You can find yakisoba noodles in Japanese markets (use just the noodles, and throw out the junky instant sauce it usually comes with). You can also boil fresh, regular ramen noodles and achieve similar great results, which is what we do in the recipe below. The secret to yakisoba is stir-frying the noodles and other ingredients with Japanese-style Worcestershire sauce and okonomiyaki sauce, so they all turn out beautifully saucy and loaded with flavor. Feel free to add more of the sauces, too, if you'd like. Yakisoba makes a great side dish, not just with okonomiyaki.

SERVES 4

4 packages (about 6 ounces each) fresh-frozen ramen noodles

2 tablespoons toasted sesame oil

½ medium Spanish onion (about 6 ounces), peeled and sliced

8 ounces fresh pork belly, thinly sliced and cut into bite-size pieces

4 ounces savoy cabbage, cut into bite-size pieces

8 ounces mung bean sprouts (moyashi)

½ cup sake

¼ cup Japanese-style Worcestershire sauce (see page 234)

¼ cup okonomiyaki sauce (see page 234) or tonkatsu sauce (page 62)

½ teaspoon freshly ground black pepper

1 tablespoon aonori (powdered nori seaweed, optional)

To prepare the ramen, fill a large stockpot with water and place over high heat. Ready 4 large bowls on a work surface. When the water comes to a boil, add the noodles. Stir the noodles for about 10 seconds, so they separate and cook evenly. Cook for about 2 minutes, until the noodles are cooked through and toothsome. When the noodles are ready, transfer them to a strainer and cool under cold running water. Set aside.

Heat the sesame oil in a large skillet or enameled cast-iron pot over medium heat. Add the onion and pork belly and cook, stirring constantly, for about 2 minutes, until the onions soften and the pork turns white. Separate the pork while you cook. Add the cabbage and sprouts and cook, stirring constantly, until the cabbage turns bright green and the spouts cook through. Add the sake, Worcestershire sauce, and okonomiyaki sauce and cook, stirring constantly, for 1 minute. Add the reserved ramen noodles. Cook, stirring constantly, until all the liquid in the skillet is absorbed, about 2 minutes. Sprinkle the black pepper and the *aonori*, on the noodles, and serve immediately.

9 DONBURI

DONBURI

Donburi is the ultimate dish for busy people: cooked, cured, or raw ingredients piled on top of a big bowl of rice, typically served with miso soup and lightly cured Japanese pickles on the side. The one bowl that does it all. It might seem straightforward enough to us, but actually eating this way, at first, was a huge leap in Japan. Sit down for a traditional meal there, whether at grandma's house or at the fanciest Kyoto *ryotei*, and we can almost guarantee you'll be served rice (even with noodles). But the rice always arrives in its own bowl, pristine and steaming white, never piled on a plate or mixed into food. So what gives with donburi?

The aforementioned busy people. Starting sometime in the eighteenth or nineteenth century, restaurants began serving donburi-style dishes. Initially dismissed as "dog food," they soon gained traction with the time-challenged (in other words, basically everyone), and donburi became hugely, enduringly popular both at home and at restaurants. Today, in fact, we count at least fifty styles of donburi, everything from classic oyakodon (opposite) to "Hawaiian" (whatever that is, but please, no pineapple!) and "taco rice" (an Okinawan specialty) to yakitori, teriyaki, and sukiyaki versions—basically any dish can be turned into donburi. In fact, there are even distinct regional styles of donburi, as you'll see in the recipes that follow.

And, oh, what recipes! All the dishes in this chapter are so easy, comforting, and fast to prepare—perfect to cook for yourself, or for your loved ones, family, and friends. You'll love the variations (we sure do), and also how the donburi rice soaks up all the beautiful flavors of the dishes and instantly becomes even more irresistible.

And did we mention the one-bowl-per-head cleanup?

OYAKODON

Let's start with the classic donburi. This dish hails from Tokyo, where it was invented in the nineteenth century. It soon entered the cooking rotation of essentially every home in the country, and for good reason. *Oyako* means "parent and child," a nod to the two main ingredients, chicken and egg. What you do is simmer chicken and onions in sweet and savory Japanese seasonings—and then add the magical flourish, eggs prepared in two layers. Two layers? *Sō des ne*, as they say in Japanese. First you set scrambled eggs over the chicken, then you cook a raw/runny layer of eggs over the set one. Then you slide everything over a steaming bowl of rice and you're good to go. So when you eat oyakodon, you get egg goodness, chicken goodness, succulent onion goodness, sweet-savory sauce goodness, and all the while the rice is happily absorbing all the amazing flavors. And don't worry—oyakodon is a snap to prepare, as you'll see below. We usually cook it one serving at a time, but we include a variation for cooking the dish for four at once. (Also, if you're not a fan of runny eggs, have no fear; we explain how to prepare oyakodon with fully cooked eggs. It's all good.)

SERVES 4

1 pound onions, peeled

1 pound boneless chicken legs or thighs (about 2 chicken legs or 4 thighs), skinned and cut into bite-size pieces

1/2 cup mirin

1/2 cup soy sauce

1/2 cup sake

1/2 cup dashi (page 161)

8 eggs

6 cups cooked Japanese white rice

1/4 cup mitsuba leaves (optional)

1/4 cup thinly sliced scallion (optional)

1/4 cup crumbled nori (optional)

Shichimi togarashi (see page 235)

Cut the onions in half lengthwise, from top to bottom (axis to axis). Cut each half into 1/4-inch slices, also cutting lengthwise.

Combine the onions, chicken, mirin, soy sauce, sake, and dashi in a saucepan and place over high heat. When the liquid comes to a boil, reduce the heat and simmer for about 5 minutes, until the chicken cooks through. Mix the ingredients occasionally as they cook.

To prepare the oyakodon one serving at a time, break 2 eggs into a bowl, and lightly beat the eggs, no more than 10 times. You want part of the yolk and whites to be lightly mixed, while other parts are still separated.

Transfer one-fourth of the chicken mixture (about 1 1/2 cups chicken, onions, and broth) to a small skillet. A 6-inch skillet works great. Place the skillet over high heat. When the liquid comes to a boil, reduce the heat so the broth is simmering.

Pour three-fourths of the egg mixture over the chicken, onions, and broth. Do not mix. Cook for about 1 minute, then add the remaining one-fourth egg over the ingredients in the skillet. Cover the skillet and cook for 30 seconds more. Turn off the

continued >

Donburi

heat, and let the oyakodon rest, covered, for 1 minute.

While the oyakodon is resting, scoop 1¹/2 cups of the cooked rice into a serving bowl. When the oyakodon is ready, uncover and slide the entire contents out of the skillet to rest on the rice. Tilt the skillet and use a spatula if necessary; the oyakodon should slide out easily. Garnish with the mitsuba, scallions, and nori. Accent with the *shichimi togarashi* to taste. Serve immediately, and repeat this preparation for the remaining servings.

Variation If you prefer your eggs cooked through, in the final step pour all the eggs over the chicken, onions, and broth in the small skillet. Cover and cook for 2 minutes. Turn off the heat and let the oyakodon rest, covered, for 1 minute.

To prepare all the servings at once, pour the entire chicken and onion mixture into a large skillet (an 11-inch cast-iron skillet works great). Place the skillet over high heat. When the broth comes to a boil, reduce the heat so the liquid is simmering. Lightly beat 8 eggs. Pour three-fourth of the eggs over the chicken mixture. Do not mix. Cook for about 1 minute. Pour the remaining one-fourth eggs over the ingredients in the skillet. Cover and cook for 30 seconds more. Turn off the heat and allow the oyakodon to rest for 1 minute. Divide the cooked rice among 4 large bowls. Use a large serving spoon to scoop the oyakodon from the skillet and place over the rice. Garnish as desired.

GYUDON

Like oyakodon, we rely on sweet and savory Japanese seasonings for this dish—but instead of chicken, we get meaty with it. Here, we simmer beef and tender onions together, then slide the mouthwatering concoction over a bowl of steaming rice. With this dish, you whip up the whole thing at once and ladle out individual portions, so it's convenient, too. Gyudon tastes best if you use a fattier cut of meat, like thinly shaved short rib or brisket. Ask your butcher to shave it, or you can find sukiyaki-style, thin-sliced beef at Japanese and Asian markets, which works perfectly for gyudon. A bit of *beni shoga* (ginger pickled bright red) on the side is a favorite accompaniment.

SERVES 4

1 medium onion (about ¾ pound), peeled

¼ cup plus 2 tablespoon soy sauce

¼ cup plus 2 tablespoons sake

¼ cup plus 2 tablespoons mirin

2 cups dashi (page 161)

2 tablespoons toasted sesame oil

1 pound shaved beef, such as sukiyaki-style beef, cut into bite-size pieces

¼ cup sugar

6 cups cooked Japanese white rice

Shichimi togarashi (see page 235)

Beni shoga (pickled ginger)

Cut the onions in half lengthwise, from top to bottom (axis to axis). Cut each half into ¼-inch slices, also cutting lengthwise.

Combine the soy sauce, sake, mirin, and dashi in a bowl, and set aside.

Heat the sesame oil in a large skillet over high heat. Add the beef and cook, stirring frequently, for about 2 minutes, until the beef browns slightly. Add the sugar, and wait 10 seconds. Add the onion and cook, stirring constantly, for about 1 minute, until the onions begin to soften. Pour the liquid mixture into the skillet. Simmer for about 5 minutes, until the ingredients cook through. While the gyudon is simmering, use a large spoon to skim off any scum and fat that appear on the surface.

While the ingredients are simmering, divide the rice among 4 large bowls. As soon as the gyudon is ready, spoon it over the rice, and serve immediately. Season with *shichimi togarashi* and *beni shoga*, as desired.

KATSUDON

Here's a marriage made in (food lovers') heaven: two all-time favorite Japanese comfort foods, tonkatsu (page 65) and donburi, served as one. The dish originated at a Tokyo restaurant near Waseda University that had prepared tonkatsu for a large party—a party that canceled their dinner at the last second. What to do with a mountain of tonkatsu? Light bulbs went off and lucky for us, katsudon was born. You cook the dish much like you would oyakodon—simmer onions in Japanese seasonings until they're succulent and sweet; top, in this case, with crispy, irresistible tonkatsu; and prepare eggs in two layers; all before sliding the ingredients over a steaming bowl of rice. Man, is this dish heavenly! So make sure to cook more than enough tonkatsu on "Tonkatsu Night," and save the leftovers for this rice bowl (tonkatsu can sit in the refrigerator for a couple of days, or freeze for up to a month). Cook katsudon one serving at a time.

SERVES 4

1 medium Spanish onion (about 12 ounces), peeled, cut in half lengthwise, and sliced

$1/2$ cup dashi (page 161)

$1/2$ cup sake

$1/2$ cup mirin

$1/2$ cup soy sauce

8 eggs

4 fillets cooked tonkatsu (page 65), each fillet cut into $1/2$-inch slices

6 cups cooked Japanese white rice

8 sprigs mitsuba (see page 235), stems and leaves coarsely chopped

Add the onion, dashi, sake, mirin, and soy sauce to a saucepan and bring to a boil over medium heat. Cook for about 5 minutes, until the onions soften.

Break 2 eggs into a bowl and lightly beat the eggs, no more than 10 times. You want part of the yolk and whites to be lightly mixed, while other parts are still separated. Set aside.

To prepare the katsudon one serving at a time, pour one-fourth of the sauce and onions into a small skillet. A 6-inch skillet works great. Place a sliced tonkatsu fillet in the sauce. Place over high heat and cook for about 30 seconds.

Pour three-fourths of the egg mixture over the tonkatsu, onions, and sauce. Do not mix. Cook for about 1 minute, then add the remaining one-fourth egg over the ingredients in the skillet. Cover the skillet and cook for 30 seconds more. Turn off the heat, and let the katsudon rest, covered, for 1 minute.

While the katsudon is resting, scoop $1 1/2$ cups of the cooked rice into a serving bowl. When the katsudon is ready, uncover, and slide entire contents out of the skillet to rest on the rice. Tilt the skillet and use a spatula if necessary; the katsudon should slide out easily. Garnish with mitsuba and serve immediately. Repeat for the remaining servings.

Donburi

TENDON

This dish is an oldie but goodie, harking way back to 1837, when a Tokyo restaurant named Misada dreamed up this food match made in culinary heaven: tempura and donburi. Wow. Not only do you layer perfect, crispy tempura over steaming rice, but you also sprinkle in tasty nibbles of tenkasu. Double wow. Tenkasu are bits of crunchy batter that separate in the oil when cooking tempura—be sure to scoop them up and save them. (Or you can find frozen tenkasu at Japanese markets.) The tenkasu are first soaked in tempura sauce, and then poured along with the sauce over the tempura and rice, adding amazing flavor bursts as you eat the dish. One of our favorites, ever.

SERVES 4

2 tablespoons sugar

1 cup dashi (page 161)

$\frac{1}{2}$ cup soy sauce

$\frac{1}{2}$ cup mirin

$\frac{1}{4}$ cup tenkasu (see headnote, page 117)

1 recipe lemon sole tempura (page 120)

1 recipe vegetable tempura (page 112)

1 recipe shrimp tempura (page 117)

6 cups cooked Japanese white rice

Add the sugar, dashi, soy sauce, and mirin to a saucepan and bring to a boil over high heat. Turn off the heat. Add the tenkasu and let it steep in the liquid for about 5 minutes.

For each serving, scoop about $1\frac{1}{2}$ cups of the cooked rice into a serving bowl.

Arrange 1 portion of fish tempura (about 4 ounces), 1 portion of vegetable tempura (about 4 ounces), and 2 pieces of shrimp tempura on top of the rice. Spoon the sauce and tenkasu over the tempura (about $\frac{1}{4}$ cup), and serve. Repeat for the remaining servings.

TEKKA DON

This donburi hails from Tokyo, where tuna once arrived to spawn in Tokyo Bay in record numbers. The tuna are gone, alas, but Tokyo residents never lost their love for this fish. Rich, luscious tuna is so delicious raw, you don't want to cook it. Instead, we lightly marinate the fish in wasabi-infused Japanese seasonings, then layer it over a bowl of rice and garnish with scallion and herby shiso. Simple, clean flavors. Fantastic.

1 pound sashimi-grade raw tuna (bigeye, ahi, or yellowfin)

½ cup soy sauce

2 tablespoon mirin

¼ teaspoon dashi powder (see headnote, page 161)

½ tablespoon wasabi

6 cups cooked Japanese rice

2 sheets nori, torn into bite-size pieces

2 tablespoons thinly sliced scallion, white and green parts

8 shiso leaves, thinly sliced

Cut the tuna into slices. Each slice should be about 2 inches long, 1 inch wide, and ⅛ inch thick. (This is approximate; if your tuna slices come out bigger or smaller, that's okay.)

Prepare an ice bath and set aside. Add the soy sauce, mirin, and dashi powder to a saucepan and bring to a boil over high heat. Turn off the heat. Place the saucepan in the ice bath to cool the liquid. When the sauce is cool, mix in the wasabi until it dissolves.

Lay the tuna slices in a single layer in a deep baking dish. Pour the marinade over the tuna and allow the fish to marinate for 10 minutes.

Divide the rice among 4 bowls. For each bowl, top with one-fourth of the nori. Lay one-fourth of the tuna slices over the nori. Sprinkle one-fourth of the scallion over the tuna. Pile one-fourth of the shiso over the scallion. Drizzle 2 tablespoons of the marinade over the shiso. Repeat with the remaining bowls, and serve.

HOKKAI-DON

The northernmost main island of Hokkaido is home to some of the richest fisheries in Japan. So it's no surprise that the local donburi, this one, is a dazzling celebration of seafood over rice. In fact, when we visited the Sapporo wholesale fish market a few years ago, we were amazed by the mind-blowing variety of seafood on display there. (Sapporo is the main city on Hokkaido.) And next to the market, we found stall after stall offering hokkai-don with the freshest ingredients possible. Needless to say, we pulled up stools and went to town—and never forgot how good this donburi tastes.

SERVES 4

8 ounces sushi-grade raw salmon, cut into 1/8-inch slices

1/2 cup soy sauce

1 tablespoon wasabi

6 cups cooked Japanese rice

16 shiso leaves

4 ounces sushi-grade raw scallops, cut in half lengthwise

4 ounces ikura (salmon roe)

4 ounces fresh uni (sea urchin)

8 sprigs mitsuba (see page 235), stems and leaves coarsely chopped

Cut the salmon into slices. Each slice should be about 2 inches long, 1 inch wide, and 1/8 inch thick. (This is approximate; if your salmon slices come out bigger or smaller, that's okay.)

Mix together the soy sauce and wasabi and set aside.

Divide the rice among 4 bowls. For each bowl, lay 4 shiso leaves over the rice. Neatly arrange one-fourth of the salmon, scallops, *ikura*, and *uni*, arranging each ingredient on top of a shiso leaf. Drizzle about 2 tablespoons of the soy sauce–wasabi mixture over the seafood. Garnish with one-fourth of the mitsuba. Repeat with the remaining bowls, and serve.

TENSHIN DON

In 1910, a customer at Rai Rai Ken, a restaurant in the old Asakusa section of Tokyo, asked the chef to whip up something tasty and tender. The chef delivered this dish. Although there's no record of the customer's reaction, it's safe to say tenshin don was a hit. This donburi has so much going for it—shiitake mushrooms, delicate crabmeat, bamboo shoots, ginger, and scallions all cooked together, then mixed with eggs to form a delicious omelet you slide over rice. The omelet is so good, by the way, don't hesitate to eat it on its own. And it's also amazing on top of chahan (page 199). The trick to this dish is a Japanese culinary technique called *ankake*, where you thicken a sauce using *katakuriko* (potato starch).

SERVES 4

1 tablespoon plus 4 teaspoons toasted sesame oil

1 (2-inch) piece ginger (about 0.8 ounce), peeled and julienned (you can finely chop if you prefer)

4 scallions, white parts only (about 2-inch length), julienned (you can finely chop if you prefer)

4 ounces bamboo shoots (fresh cooked or canned), rinsed and julienned (you can finely chop if you prefer)

8 ounces shiitake mushrooms, stemmed and sliced

8 ounces crabmeat (canned), drained and flaked

8 eggs

¼ teaspoon salt

¼ teaspoon plus pinch ground white or black pepper

¼ cup sugar

1 cup torigara stock (page 25)

3 tablespoons soy sauce

¼ cup Japanese rice vinegar

2 tablespoons sake

1 tablespoon katakuriko (potato starch) mixed with 1 tablespoon water

6 cups cooked Japanese white rice

2 tablespoons chopped scallion

Heat 1 tablespoon of the sesame oil in a skillet over medium heat. Add the ginger, julienned scallions, bamboo shoots, and shiitake mushrooms. Cook, stirring constantly, for about 2 minutes, until the ingredients soften. Transfer the ingredients to a bowl. Add the crabmeat, and mix together.

In a separate bowl, mix the eggs, salt, and ¼ teaspoon pepper. Add to the crab mixture, combine well, and set aside.

To make the *ankake*, add the sugar, *torigara* stock, soy sauce, vinegar, sake, and remaining pinch of pepper to a saucepan. Place over medium heat and bring to a boil. Reduce the heat to low and add the *katakuriko* mixture. Cook for 15 seconds, stirring well to combine and thicken. Turn off the heat.

To prepare the tenshin don, one serving at a time, preheat a small skillet over medium heat. (A 6-inch skillet works

continued >

Tenshin Don,
continued

great.) Add 1 teaspoon of the sesame oil, and wait 10 seconds. Add one-fourth of the crab-egg mixture. Use a spatula to push together the crab-egg mixture to form an omelet. Cook for 2 minutes. Flip the omelet and cook for 1 minute more. Transfer the crab omelet to a plate. Repeat to make 3 more omelets.

Divide the cooked rice among 4 bowls. Top each bowl with an omelet. Pour one-fourth of the *ankake* over each omelet. Garnish with the chopped scallions and serve immediately.

CHŪKA DON

Now we cross the Sea of Japan to China for don-buri inspiration. (*Chūka* is the Japanese word for "China.") Indeed, this popular dish is chock-full of typically Chinese ingredients, like pork belly and quail eggs, and vegetables like napa cabbage and mushrooms. You can go hardcore and add wood ear mushrooms (soak first, then add with the carrots and onions) or snow peas (add with the bamboo), if you'd like. Be sure to cook the vegetables until they're just firm—you want them to keep their natural texture and flavors, not turn into mush. As with tenshin don, we thicken this dish with *ankake*. You can find quail eggs at Chinese markets (they're also sold pre-boiled, in cans), or substitute with 1/2 hard-boiled chicken egg per serving. If you like your don-buri spicy, feel free to add a dab of *tobanjan*.

SERVES 4

8 quail eggs (optional)

8 ounces fresh pork belly, thinly sliced and cut into bite-size pieces

1 tablespoon plus 1/4 cup sake

1 teaspoon freshly grated ginger

Pinch plus 1 teaspoon salt

Pinch ground white or black pepper

1/2 medium onion (about 6 ounces), peeled

1 small carrot (about 2 ounces), peeled and sliced on an angle

1 1/2 cups torigara stock (page 25)

1 tablespoon soy sauce

1 tablespoon toasted sesame oil

4 ounces bamboo shoots (precooked or canned), rinsed and thinly sliced

8 ounces napa cabbage, sliced into bite-size pieces

4 ounces shiitake mushrooms, stems removed and sliced

1 (1-inch) piece ginger (about 0.4 ounce), peeled and thinly sliced

1 tablespoon katakuriko (potato starch) mixed with 1 tablespoon water

6 cups cooked Japanese white rice

Japanese white pepper, to taste

To prepare the quail eggs, place them in a small saucepan and cover with water. Place over high heat and bring to a boil. Reduce the heat so the water simmers gently, and cook for 5 minutes. Transfer the saucepan to a sink and cool in cold running water. When the eggs are cool to the touch, peel and set aside.

Add the pork belly, 1 tablespoon of the sake, grated ginger, pinch salt, and pepper to a bowl. Mix together well and set aside. Coarsely chop the onion into pieces about 1/2 inch thick. Combine with the carrot in a bowl and set aside. Mix together the *torigara* stock, remaining 1/4 cup sake, soy sauce, and remaining 1 teaspoon salt and set aside.

Heat the sesame oil in a large skillet over high heat (an 11-inch cast-iron skillet or wok works great). Add the pork and cook, stirring frequently, for about 2 minutes, until the pork begins to turn white. Add the carrots and onions, and cook, stirring constantly, for 2 minutes more. Add the bamboo shoots, napa cabbage, shiitakes, and sliced ginger and cook, stirring frequently, for 1 minute more. Pour in the liquid mixture. Cook for 3 minutes. Add the *katakuriko* mixture, and stir to thicken the dish. Cook for 10 seconds and turn off the heat.

Divide the cooked rice among 4 bowls. Spoon the chūka don over the rice. Top with 2 quail eggs. Season with Japanese white pepper, to taste. Serve immediately.

MABO DON

Here's another Chinese-inspired donburi that's huge in Japan, this one a riff off that classic of Sichuan cooking, *mabodofu*. In fact, *mabodofu* was introduced to Japan by a chef and Sichuan native named Chin Kenmin, who opened the first Sichuanese restaurant in Tokyo in the 1950s, and then popularized the cuisine on Japanese television. It wasn't long before mabo tofu, as it's known in Japan, became fodder for donburi. Like the original *mabodofu*, the Japanese version is cooked with tofu and ground pork, but in Japan it's not served nearly as hot as it is in Sichuan. Substitute ground beef for the pork, if you'd like. And you can also garnish this dish with coarsely chopped cilantro leaves, for an added Chinese touch, and a sprinkling of sansho, an intensely aromatic Japanese seasoning that's related to Sichuan pepper.

SERVES 4

1 package (1 pound) firm tofu, cut in half lengthwise

1 (2-inch) piece ginger (about 0.8 ounce), peeled and minced

2 cloves garlic, peeled and minced

3 scallions, white parts only (about 2-inch length), minced

1 cup torigara stock (page 25)

2 tablespoons sake

1 tablespoon soy sauce

2 teaspoons sugar

2 tablespoons Sendai miso or other aged, red miso (see page 234)

2 tablespoons toasted sesame oil

1 tablespoon water

1 tablespoon katakuriko (potato starch)

1 tablespoon Japanese rice vinegar

8 ounces ground pork

2 teaspoons tobanjan (see page 236)

6 cups cooked Japanese white rice

¼ cup coarsely chopped cilantro leaves (optional)

Sansho

Place the tofu slices on a work surface and lay a clean kitchen towel or cheesecloth over them. Place a weight on top of the tofu, such as a heavy skillet, for 30 minutes to press out any excess liquid. When the tofu is ready, cut it into 1-inch cubes and set aside.

In a bowl, mix together the ginger, garlic, and white parts of the scallion, and set aside. Mix together the *torigara* stock, sake, soy sauce, sugar, and miso in a bowl and set aside. Mix together 1 tablespoon of the sesame oil, the water, the *katakuriko*, and the vinegar in a small bowl and set aside.

Heat the remaining 1 tablespoon sesame oil in a large skillet over high heat (an 11-inch cast-iron skillet or wok works great). Add the pork and the ginger, garlic, scallion mixture, and the *tobanjan*. Cook for about 2 minutes. Use a fork to break up the chopped meat and stir the ingredients. Add the liquid mixture. When the liquid comes to a boil, reduce the heat to medium, so the liquid simmers. Add the tofu and cook for 3 minutes. Add the *katakuriko* mixture, and stir to thicken the dish. Cook for 30 seconds more.

Divide the cooked rice among 4 bowls and spoon the mabo tofu over. Garnish with the chopped cilantro and season with *sansho*, to taste.

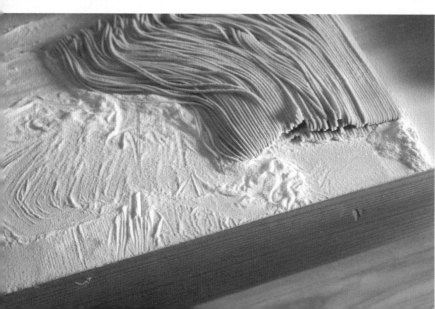

10 SOBA

SOBA

Japanese have been slurping soba for hundreds of years. The first mention of this iconic Japanese noodle appeared in a book in 1706; the first recorded soba restaurant popped up in Tokyo that same century. In fact, the noodle is closely associated with the citizens of Edo, as Tokyo was originally called, who made it a habit to gather at neighborhood soba shops and wash down their meals with more than a few glasses of sake. Even today it's considered "Tokyo's noodle," with udon, page 174, associated with Osaka. But soba is also firmly embedded in greater Japanese culture. It's a New Year's custom to eat soba for good fortune and long life. And when Japanese move to a new home, there is an old tradition of neighbors presenting them with soba as a welcoming gift.

Soba is made from buckwheat flour and water, with a little wheat flour often added to give the dough more elasticity. The result is a noodle that's toothsome, nutty, and incredibly appealing. Soba is served hot or cold, in a broth or with a dipping sauce, and often paired with tempura, a double whammy that's totally irresistible (see page 166).

Traditionally, soba dough is mixed, kneaded, and rolled out using three or more long pins (about four feet across) until it's cardboard-thin, then folded into layers like a bolt of fabric, and cut into noodles using a huge, heavy *soba kiri* (soba knife). Watching a soba master make noodles is an awesome spectacle to behold. And you can still witness it firsthand at numerous soba shops in Japan, where the master typically performs the deft noodle cutting in front of customers.

Soba, like lots of foods in Japan, is often elevated to high art, but like the soba shops of old Edo, it's also still very much local, neighborhood fare. (But even in tiny neighborhood soba shops, the master often hand cuts the noodles.) And in train stations and on street corners of the old parts of Tokyo and other cities, you can still find "standing" soba shops where patrons elbow up to the counter for a quick bowl of noodles they slurp while, well, on their feet.

Soba is also a standard of Japanese home cooking, using dried or flash-frozen soba that's available at any Japanese or Asian market here (and increasingly at our good ol' all-purpose supermarkets, too), which is delicious. The recipes that follow are all simple, easy home cooking that will get you hooked on this fantastic noodle. In fact, we know one plucky nonagenarian—one of the Japanese innovators who originally introduced sushi to America, believe it or not—who eats soba for breakfast every day and claims it's what keeps him healthy and vigorous. Who are we to argue?

DASHI Master Recipe

This is a foolproof recipe for an all-purpose dashi. *Dashi* is the Japanese word for "stock," but it also refers to this particular version, made from kombu (a type of super umami-rich, naturally preserved kelp) and dried, shaved bonito—considered a fundamental building block of traditional Japanese cuisine. You'll need dashi for some of the soba dishes in this chapter. Use it hot off the stove, at room temperature, or cold. It can keep in the freezer for up to 2 months. Keep in mind, too, that an alternative to making dashi from scratch is using "dashi packs" or all-natural dashi powder, which are both terrific. The packs look like giant teabags you stick in water and heat; follow the package instructions. The all-natural powder has also become more available in America in the past few years. It's super easy to use; just dissolve in hot water, following package instructions. But check the label carefully to make sure your dashi powder is an all-natural version, not one with additives and other junk.

MAKES ABOUT 6 CUPS

8 cups plus 2 tablespoons water

2 (6-inch) pieces kombu

1½ ounces dried, shaved bonito (about 3 packed cups)

Add 8 cups of the water and the kombu to a large stockpot and let it steep for 30 minutes.

Place the stockpot over medium heat and bring to a boil. Remove the kombu. Add the remaining 2 tablespoons water to slightly reduce the liquid's temperature. Add the bonito and stir it once to mix it in. As soon as the liquid comes to a boil again, decrease the heat to low and simmer for 5 minutes. Remove any scum that appears on the surface, which can affect flavor.

Turn off the heat and let the liquid steep for 15 minutes. Strain the liquid through a fine sieve or cheesecloth. Don't squeeze the bonito flakes. Discard the bonito flakes after using.

KAESHI Master Recipe

Kaeshi is the flavoring base you use to make both soba dipping sauce and soba broth. This umami-rich, sweet-savory concentrate gets better with time, so leave it in the refrigerator for at least three days before using, and always keep some handy for making soba on the fly, any time your heart desires.

MAKES ABOUT 2½ CUPS

2 cups soy sauce

½ cup mirin

3 tablespoons sugar

Add the ingredients to a saucepan and bring to a boil over high heat. Turn off the heat and allow the kaeshi to come to room temperature. Refrigerate for 3 days to give the flavors time to mingle and deepen. Kaeshi can keep in the refrigerator for up to 1 month.

How to Cook Dried Soba

There are many varieties of dried soba sold in America, at Japanese and Asian markets, and sometimes at regular supermarkets. Look for packaged dried soba where the noodles are already portioned into 100-gram (about 3½-ounce) individual servings. Each serving is wrapped with a thin plastic band that you pull off before cooking, making it easy to get the quantity right. To prepare four servings, bring a pot with at least 3 quarts of unsalted water to a boil over high heat. (Boil the soba in plenty of water to give the noodles room to cook evenly.) Add four servings of soba (400 grams), making sure to pull off the plastic band from each serving. Swirl the noodles with chopsticks to separate them. Check package instructions for exact cooking times, but here are general guidelines: For cold soba dishes, we usually cook the noodles for about 4½ minutes; for hot soba dishes, we usually cook the noodles for about 4 minutes (they'll cook more in the hot broth). (Cooking time depends on the type of soba, the thickness of the noodles, and other factors.) Test the noodles for doneness by pulling one out of the pot, running it under cold water, and biting into it. The soba should be toothsome and cooked through, not mushy. Be careful not to overcook the noodles. When they're ready, strain the noodles in a colander. For cold noodles, cool the soba under cold, running water. For hot noodles, serve immediately. Or if you're not serving immediately, cool the soba under cold, running water and reheat just before eating by plunging the noodles into boiling water for 10 seconds, swirling constantly.

Slurp!

When eating soba (or any other Japanese noodle, in fact), throw out everything you've learned from Miss Manners—and make sure you slurp loud, slurp proud! Besides sounding like you're enjoying yourself, slurping has three practical effects. If you're eating hot soba, slurping helps cool the noodles as they approach your lips. Also, regardless of whether you eat soba hot or cold, slurping helps you suck up broth or dipping sauce along with your noodles, which makes the whole experience so much more flavorful and delicious. Finally, slurping pulls up air with the noodles and aerates them, creating more fragrance, which adds to your sensory taste experience. (And yes, wine geeks, it's the same effect as sucking air when tasting vino.) So slurp away!

MORI SOBA

How do you know if a soba master is worth his or her buckwheat flour? With this dish, which is comprised of just cold soba, dipping sauce, and garnishes— that's it. So the soba's got to be perfect—there's nowhere for the chef to hide. Luckily for us mortals, the pressure's not nearly as great as it is for the master. So we can just enjoy this simple, elemental soba, which is fantastic for summertime. To make the dipping sauce (called tsuyu), the classic proportion is 4 parts dashi to 1 part kaeshi. You can make the dipping sauce the day before and cool it in the refrigerator overnight, or use an ice bath right after you prepare it.

SERVES 4

2 cups dashi (page 161)
½ cup kaeshi (page 162)
2 tablespoons mirin
4 servings soba (see page 162)
¼ cup finely sliced scallion

To prepare the cold soba dipping sauce, add the dashi, kaeshi, and mirin to a saucepan and bring to a boil over medium heat. Allow the dipping sauce to come to room temperature. Refrigerate for about 1 hour to cool and let the flavors combine.

Right before serving, cook the soba (see page 162). Drain the soba in a colander, then place the colander with the soba in a large bowl, and rinse the noodles under cold, running water until the noodles are cooled. (The bowl will also fill with cold water, which will help cool the noodles.)

To serve, divide the soba among 4 plates, and pour the dipping sauce into 4 small cups, with the 1 tablespoon scallion on the side of each plate. To eat, add the scallions to the dipping sauce. Dip the soba into the sauce and slurp up with the scallions.

Soba

COLD SOBA VARIATIONS

Once you demonstrate your mori soba mojo, don't rest on your laurels: try this pair of wonderful variations.

Zaru Soba

Zaru soba *literally means "basket soba," because it's often served in Japan in a dish-shaped basket of woven bamboo. We simply add nori (needle-cut or shredded papery sheets of seaweed) and wasabi to create this classic variation of mori soba (page 165).*

¼ cup needle-cut (or shredded) nori
¼ cup finely sliced scallion
2 teaspoons wasabi

Prepare the mori soba following the recipe on page 165, but add garnishes. Divide the nori, scallion, and wasabi among 4 small plates. To eat, add the garnishes to the dipping sauce, to taste. Dip the soba into the sauce and slurp up with the garnishes.

Zaru Soba with Tempura

Another super popular way to enjoy zaru soba is to serve it with shrimp and vegetable tempura on the side.

1 recipe shrimp tempura (page 117)
1 recipe vegetable tempura (page 112)
Shichimi togarashi (see page 235)

Prepare the zaru soba variation above. To eat, dip the tempura into the soba noodle dipping sauce to eat. Season with *shichimi togarashi*, to taste.

KAKE SOBA

Now on to kake soba, or soba noodles served in a comforting, delicious hot broth. You make the broth (also called tsuyu) using a proportion of 8 parts dashi to 1 part kaeshi—in a hot broth the flavors are more pronounced than in a cold dipping sauce, so you need less kaeshi. There are so many styles of hot soba to keep you warm and satisfied all winter long (see "Hot Soba Variations," page 168). Here's the basic recipe.

SERVES 4

broth
6 cups dashi (page 161)
½ cup plus 2 tablespoons kaeshi (page 162)
6 tablespoons mirin

4 servings soba (see page 162)
4 teaspoons finely sliced negi or scallion
Shichimi togarashi (see page 234)

To prepare the hot soba broth, add the dashi, kaeshi, and mirin to a saucepan and bring to a boil over high heat. Reduce the heat to low to keep the broth warm.

Right before serving, cook the soba (see page 162).

Divide the soba among 4 bowls. Pour the broth over the noodles. Top each bowl with 1 teaspoon of *negi* and season with *shichimi togarashi*, to taste. Serve immediately.

Soba-Yu

In traditional Japanese soba shops, noodles are all cooked in the same monster pot of water. After a bunch of orders, that water transforms into something amazing, the liquid absorbing the very essence of soba. At soba joints, this fortified water, called soba-yu (*yu* means "hot water"), is poured into the remaining dipping sauce after a meal, and customers drink the concoction as a satisfying, intensely flavored finale to their noodles. If you can save the cooking water from your soba making, try pouring some into your remaining dipping sauce and enjoy (never drink dipping sauce straight—way too strong).

HOT SOBA VARIATIONS

Here are some great variations to basic kake soba (page 167). For *chikara soba,* add toasted mochi on top of each serving. *Okame soba* calls for adding slices of *kamaboko* (steamed white fish cake). With *nori soba,* divide one sheet of nori per bowl into four pieces and float them on top of the broth; to eat, wrap the soba with the nori. Here are more variations.

Tempura Soba

Like zaru soba with tempura (page 166), this amazing dish is a classic of Japanese cuisine.

1 recipe shrimp tempura (page 117)
1 recipe vegetable tempura (page 112)
Shichimi togarashi (see page 234)

Prepare the kake soba as directed on page 167. Arrange the tempura on top of the kake soba in the bowl, or serve on the side. Season with *shichimi togarashi,* to taste. If you serve the tempura on the side, dip it into the hot broth to eat.

Tsukumi Soba

Here you add raw eggs to the soba, which poach slightly in the hot broth. Use the freshest eggs you can find.

4 eggs
4 teaspoons finely sliced scallions
Shichimi togarashi (see page 234)

Prepare the kake soba as directed on page 167. Divide the soba among 4 bowls. Carefully pour the hot broth over the noodles. For each bowl, gently slide a raw egg into the soup. Top each bowl with 1 teaspoon of scallions and season with *shichimi togarashi,* to taste. Serve immediately. To eat, mix together or slurp up the egg separately, your choice.

Tanuki Soba

This simple but tasty variation uses bits of fried tempura batter called tenkasu (see page 115) to add crispy texture.

¼ cup tenkasu (see page 115)

Prepare the kake soba as directed on page 167. Sprinkle the tenkasu over each bowl, and serve.

NATTO SOBA

Natto is fermented soybeans, a specialty of Kanto, or the eastern side of Japan. We love natto, which has an appealing nutty flavor. But, fair warning: not everyone's a fan. Its sticky, slippery texture (a bit like raw okra) can be off-putting. If you're in the "love natto" camp, this cold soba dish is really lovely, especially because the natto is paired with tangy *umeboshi* (a kind of sour and salty pickled Japanese apricot), which is very refreshing in the summer. Add more *umeboshi* to this dish, if you like.

4 cups dashi (page 161)

½ cup kaeshi (page 163)

1 tablespoon mirin

8 small umeboshi (about ¾ inch diameter), pitted and chopped

4 packs (50 grams each) natto

4 servings soba (see page 162)

8 shiso leaves, thinly sliced

¼ cup thinly sliced scallion

¼ cup needle-cut (or shredded) nori

Add the dashi, kaeshi, and mirin to a saucepan and bring to a boil over high heat. Allow the dipping sauce to come to room temperature. Add the *umeboshi*. Refrigerate for about 1 hour to cool and let the flavors combine. (You can also prepare this the day before and refrigerate overnight.)

Add 1 pack of natto to a small bowl. (Discard any sauce packets that might come with the natto.) Using chopsticks, vigorously whip the natto in a circular motion for about 30 seconds, until the natto becomes loose and liquidy. Set aside. Repeat with the remaining packages.

Right before serving, cook the soba (see page 162). Drain the soba in a colander, then place the colander with the soba in a large bowl and rinse the noodles under cold, running water until the noodles are cooled. (The bowl will also fill with cold water, which will help cool the noodles.)

Divide the soba among 4 bowls. Top each bowl with 1 serving of natto. Pour the dipping sauce with *umeboshi* over the soba and natto in the bowls. Top each bowl with equal parts shiso leaves, scallions, and nori, in that order, piling one garnish on top of the other. Serve immediately.

Soba

KAMO NANBAN SOBA

This is one of our very favorite dishes, soba in hot broth served with tender slices of duck breast. It's accented with wasabi, which just pops the flavor of the bird. Amazing. Be sure to prepare the duck breast tender and rare; otherwise, it'll become tough and tasteless if overcooked. Keep in mind, too, that the duck will cook slightly more in the hot soup, another reason to keep it rare. You'll see that we sauté the *negi* in this dish in duck fat, which adds even more incredible flavor to the soba.

SERVES 4

6 cups dashi (page 161)

¾ cup kaeshi (page 162)

6 tablespoons mirin

2 duck breasts (about 1½ pounds total)

Salt

2 negi (see page 235), white parts only, sliced into 1½-inch pieces

4 servings soba (see page 162)

¼ cup thinly sliced negi or scallion

4 teaspoons wasabi

Shichimi togarashi (see page 234)

To prepare the hot soba broth, add the dashi, kaeshi, and mirin to a saucepan and bring to a boil over high heat. Remove from the heat and set aside.

To prepare the duck, trim off excess fat from the duck breasts. Cut crisscross notches about ⅛ inch deep into the duck's skin, so the skin doesn't shrink when cooking and the layer of fat under the skin renders easier. Season the duck with salt on both sides.

Preheat a dry skillet over medium heat. Lay the duck breasts in the skillet, skin side down. Cook for about 2 minutes, until the skin browns and fat begins to render. Turn the duck, and reduce the heat to low. Cook for 3 more minutes and turn again, so the skin side is again down. Cook for 2 minutes and transfer the duck to a cutting board. The duck will be cooked rare.

Pour out the fat that has accumulated in the skillet and discard. Return the skillet to the heat. Add the 1½-inch pieces *negi* and cook for about 1 minute, until the *negi* caramelizes slightly. Transfer to a plate.

Thinly slice the duck, and set aside.

Cook the soba (see page 162).

Add the duck slices and *negi* to the broth. Return the broth to a boil over medium heat. Turn off the heat.

Divide the soba noodles among 4 bowls. Use a ladle to pour the broth over the soba. Use chopsticks or tongs to pick up the duck slices and *negi* from the saucepan, and arrange them over the soba. Garnish each bowl with about 1 tablespoon sliced *negi* and 1 teaspoon wasabi. Season with *shichimi togarashi*, to taste.

11 UDON

UDON

Thick, chewy, and toothsome, udon are delectable wheat flour noodles that cry out "comfort food." And they've been comforting Japanese for hundreds of years; in fact, a Buddhist priest is believed to have introduced udon from China way, way back in the eighth century. Associated with the city of Osaka and its environs, udon often plays second viola to its more glamorous noodle cousin, soba. But down-home udon is extremely popular in Japan, slurped as a quick meal at train station counter joints and eaten regularly at home. We love udon, too, and in this chapter we share classic recipes for every season.

There are several varieties of udon, but for our dishes, we stick to "Sanuki" udon: fat, extra-thick, extra-chewy noodles that hail from the rural city of Takamatsu on rugged, breathtaking Shikoku, the smallest of the country's main islands, which sits astride Japan's Inland Sea. As every udon fanatic (and even nonfanatic) in Japan knows, Takamatsu sits smack in the center of the Sanuki universe. Hundreds of udon joints dot this diminutive burg; "udon taxis," complete with huge plastic replicas of udon bowls lashed to their roofs, ferry passengers from shop to shop; and the city hosts a huge udon festival every year, where, besides merriment (and possible overeating), noodles are consecrated at local temples. Holy stuff. Udon cooks in Takamatsu ply their craft just as reverently, kneading the dough by stomping on it with their stockinged feet, interestingly, before carefully hand-cutting and cooking the noodles. Lucky for us, we don't have to stomp on dough to enjoy Sanuki udon, as they're widely available here.

UDON TSUYU

Master Recipe

Udon is usually served in its own special broth, or tsuyu, that calls for *usukuchi* soy sauce (see page 235), a lighter colored, saltier variety than standard soy sauce that marries so perfectly with the dense noodles.

SERVES 4

6 cups dashi (page 161)

½ cup mirin

½ cup usukuchi soy sauce (see page 235)

1 teaspoon salt

Add the dashi, mirin, *usukuchi* soy sauce, and salt to a saucepan and bring to a boil over high heat. Turn off the heat and set aside. Reheat before serving, or it can keep in the refrigerator for up to 5 days (any longer, and the flavor dissipates).

How to Cook Fresh-Frozen Udon

For our udon recipes, we use flash-frozen Sanuki udon, which is found in the freezer section of Japanese and Asian markets. This udon is precooked and rinsed, then frozen into single-serving bricks (each brick is typically 250 grams, or 8.8 ounces). To cook, bring a large pot of water to a boil over high heat. Drop the bricks into the boiling water and swirl with chopsticks. As soon as the water boils again, the udon is done. Strain and use in the recipes that follow. (Alternatively, you can use dried Sanuki udon; follow package instructions to prepare. Use about 100 grams, or 3.5 ounces, of dried udon per serving.)

KITSUNE UDON

As any child—and thankful parent—in Japan can tell you, this dish is one of their favorites. Here, abura-age, deep-fried slices of tofu, are seasoned in a sweet-savory sauce that no kid can resist, and floated over udon and broth. Tasty fried tofu, noodles, soup: sound simple enough? Well, we told you parents are thankful! The name of this dish is the Japanese word for "fox," whose russet-colored coat is thought to resemble the tofu. Abura-age is sold in packets at Japanese and some Asian markets. Before using, pour boiling water over the abura-age first to rid it of any excess oil from deep-frying, then you cook it.

SERVES 4

4 pieces (about 1/2 ounce each) abura-age

1/2 cup water

2 tablespoons mirin

2 tablespoons soy sauce

1 recipe udon tsuyu (page 175)

4 bricks (8.8 ounces each) fresh-frozen udon or 4 packages (3.5 ounces each) dried Sanuki udon

1/4 cup thinly sliced scallion

To prepare the abura-age, place it in a bowl and pour enough boiling water to cover. Use chopsticks to mix the abura-age to eliminate excess oil. Transfer the abura-age to a colander and rinse under cold, running water. When the abura-age has cooled, squeeze excess water from each slice with your hands. Place the abura-age on a cutting board and cut in half, crosswise.

Add the prepared abura-age, water, mirin, and soy sauce to a saucepan and bring to a boil over medium heat. Cook for about 5 minutes to infuse the abura-age with flavor. After cooking for 1 minute, turn the abura-age. Cook for 2 minutes and turn

again. Cook for 2 minutes more and turn a final time. The abura-age is ready when at least half of the liquid has been absorbed by the tofu.

Prepare the tsuyu (see page 175) and keep it warm over low heat.

Prepare the fresh-frozen udon (see page 175), divide among 4 bowls, and set aside.

Pour the hot tsuyu over the noodles. Add 2 halves of the abura-age to each bowl. Garnish each bowl with 1 tablespoon of scallions, and serve.

NIKU UDON

Niku means "meat," and in this style of udon you top noodles and broth with shaved beef that's been marinated, then caramelized in a skillet. The sharpness of the sliced *negi* adds contrast and bite. Like all udon dishes, it's simple but so mouthwatering. In fact, restaurants across Japan specialize in just this dish.

SERVES 4

¼ cup sake

¼ cup sugar

¼ cup soy sauce

1 pound shaved beef (look for sukiyaki beef at Asian markets, or ask your butcher), cut into bite-size pieces

6 cups udon tsuyu (page 175)

4 bricks (8.8 ounces each) fresh-frozen udon or 4 packages (3.5 ounces each) dried Sanuki udon

1 negi or scallion, thinly sliced on an angle

Shichimi togarashi (see page 235)

Make a marinade by adding the sake, sugar, and soy sauce to a large bowl, and mixing together well. Add the beef and mix together with your hands, making sure all the meat is coated well. Marinate the beef for about 10 minutes.

Preheat a dry skillet. Add the beef with the entire marinade mixture to the skillet. Spread out the beef in the skillet so it cooks evenly. Cook for about 5 minutes over high heat, until almost all the liquid in the skillet has evaporated. Turn off the heat.

Prepare the tsuyu (see page 175) and keep it warm over low heat.

Prepare the fresh-frozen udon (see page 175), divide among 4 bowls, and set aside.

Pour the hot tsuyu over the udon. Divide the beef among the 4 bowls, placing it on top of the noodles. Garnish with the *negi* and season with the *shichimi togarashi*, to taste. Serve immediately.

MISO NIKOMI UDON

SERVES 4

If you want to warm up on a freezing winter day, head directly to the kitchen and whip up this hearty udon for family and friends. Here, udon is simmered with pork, eggs, and mushrooms in a deeply savory miso broth. So satisfying when it's cold, or worse, outside. Serve this dish tableside for the full effect. Kamaboko is a steamed Japanese fish cake. If you can't find it, don't worry, just delete it from the recipe. We like to cook this dish in an earthenware hot pot, but an enameled cast-iron pot like a Le Creuset works great, too (or any pot you have; don't sweat it).

4 bricks (8.8 ounces each) fresh-frozen udon or 4 packages (3.5 ounces each) dried Sanuki udon

8 cups dashi (see page 161), at room temperature

¾ cup Sendai miso or other red miso (see page 234)

½ cup mirin

8 ounces pork shoulder, thinly sliced

1 package (150 grams) kamaboko, cut into ½-inch-thick slices

4 ounces napa cabbage leaves, cut into bite-size pieces

4 ounces shiitake mushrooms (about 4 mushrooms), stems removed and sliced

1 package (200 grams) enoki mushrooms, trimmed and separated

2 negi or scallions, white and green parts, sliced on an angle into 2-inch pieces

4 eggs

Prepare the fresh-frozen udon (see page 175), and set aside.

Add the dashi, miso, and mirin to the work bowl of a blender. Pulse for about 1 minute until the mixture becomes smooth. Depending on the size of your blender, you may want to do this in batches.

Place the udon on the bottom of a hot pot. Add the pork, kamaboko, napa cabbage, shiitake, enoki, and *negi* on top of the udon, arranging each ingredient into a separate, neat bunch. Pour the miso mixture into the hot pot.

Cover the hot pot and place over medium heat. When the liquid comes to a boil, reduce the heat to low and simmer for about 5 minutes. Uncover, and crack the eggs into the hot pot, being careful not to break the yolks. Cover again and simmer for about 3 more minutes to poach the eggs.

Transfer the hot pot to the dining table and rest it on a heatproof trivet. Uncover and serve.

NABEYAKI UDON

Like miso nikomi udon (page 179), this udon dish is cooked in a hot pot and has been battled-tested on the coldest of winter nights. Here, the udon simmers in a hot pot filled with savory broth, chicken, abura-age (deep-fried tofu slices), spinach, and other delectables. Like its miso cousin, it's also über-satisfying and can be cooked in an earthenware hot pot, an enameled cast-iron pot like a Le Creuset, or as an individual dish.

4 bricks (8.8 ounces each) fresh-frozen udon or 4 packages (3.5 ounces each) dried Sanuki udon

2 slices abura-age (see page 177)

1 package (150 grams) kamaboko (see page 179), cut into ½-inch-thick slices

1 chicken leg (about 10 ounces), boned, skinned, and cut into bite-size pieces (8 ounces of meat, if buying a boneless leg)

4 ounces shiitake mushrooms (about 4 mushrooms), stems removed and sliced

2 negi, white and green parts, sliced on an angle into 2-inch pieces

½ bunch spinach (about 8 ounces), trimmed, cleaned, boiled, and cooled in ice water

6 cups udon tsuyu (page 175)

4 eggs

Prepare the fresh-frozen udon (see page 175), and set aside.

To prepare the abura-age, place the abura-age in a bowl and pour enough boiling water to cover. Use chopsticks to mix the abura-age to eliminate excess oil. Transfer the abura-age to a colander and rinse under cold, running water. When the abura-age has cooled, squeeze excess water from each slice with your hands. Cut into triangles, and set aside.

Place the udon on the bottom of a hot pot. Add the abura-age, kamaboko, chicken, shiitake, *negi*, and spinach on top of the udon, arranging each ingredient into a separate, neat bunch. Pour the udon tsuyu into the hot pot until the vessel is three-fourths full.

Cover the hot pot and place over medium heat. When the liquid comes to a boil, reduce the heat to low and simmer for about 5 minutes. Uncover, and crack the eggs into the hot pot, being careful not to break the yolks. Cover again and simmer for about 3 more minutes to poach the eggs.

Transfer the hot pot to the dining table and rest it on a heatproof trivet. Uncover and serve.

UDON-SUKI

Sukiyaki is a beloved celebration food in Japan, a hot pot made with shaved beef and vegetables. Another popular version of this dish is this hot pot, centering on chewy udon noodles. Here we add seafood and chicken, a combination that creates amazing mouthwatering flavor (from how the umami compounds in these ingredients combine), and simmer the ingredients in a delicious *warishita*, or umami-amped seasoning sauce. A whole lot of umami here. We use *usukuchi* soy sauce in this recipe, the light-colored soy sauce of the Osaka and Kyoto region, which won't overwhelm the delicate seafood. You can accent with *yuzu kosho* (see page 236), too, if you'd like.

SERVES 4

4 cups dashi (page 235)

½ cup mirin

½ cup usukuchi soy sauce (see page 235)

1 chicken leg (about 8 ounces), boned, skinned, and cut into bite-size pieces

2 bricks (8.8 ounces each) fresh-frozen udon or 2 packages (3.5 ounces each) dried Sanuki udon

8 ounces napa cabbage, sliced

½ package (about 8 ounces) firm tofu, cut into 4 pieces

4 littleneck clams

4 jumbo shrimp, with head on

4 sea scallops

8 ounces red snapper or sea bass fillet, cut into 1-inch slices

1 negi, sliced on an angle into 2-inch pieces

Half package (200 grams) enoki mushrooms, trimmed and pulled apart

1 package (100 grams) shimeji mushrooms, trimmed and pulled apart

½ medium carrot (about 2 ounces), peeled, cut into 2-inch pieces, then thinly sliced lengthwise

½ cup thinly sliced scallion, white and green parts

Shichimi togarashi (see page 235)

Prepare the *warishita* by combining the dashi, mirin, and soy sauce in a bowl. Set aside.

Fill a saucepan with water and bring it to a boil over high heat. Add the chicken and blanch for 1 minute. Strain the chicken in a colander and cool under running water.

Place the frozen udon blocks on the bottom of a hot pot. Add the cabbage over the noodles. On top of the cabbage, add the tofu, clams, shrimp, scallops, red snapper, *negi*, enoki mushrooms, shimeji mushrooms, and carrots, arranging each ingredient in a separate, neat bunch. Pour in the reserved *warishita*.

Cover the hot pot and bring it to a boil over high heat. Decrease the heat to medium, uncover the pot, and simmer for 10 minutes.

Transfer the hot pot to the dining table. Serve the hot pot ingredients and broth in small bowls. Garnish with the scallions and season with the *shichimi togarashi*, to taste.

CURRY UDON

SERVES 4

Japanese curry and udon are so popular in Japan that of course, they're cooked together. These noodles, drenched in a mouthwatering curry with pork and onions, are definitely a keeper. You'll notice that we use soba broth to prepare this udon dish. Why? We need the more powerful flavor of the soba tsuyu to stand up to the heady flavor of the curry. You can also substitute the pork with chicken, if you'd like. Use 1 pound sliced boneless chicken, white or dark parts.

4 bricks (8.8 ounces each) fresh-frozen udon or 4 packages (3.5 ounces each) dried Sanuki udon

1 tablespoons sesame oil

1 pound fresh pork belly, thinly sliced and cut into bite-size pieces

1 medium Spanish onion (about 12 ounces), peeled and sliced

3 tablespoons curry powder

1 recipe kake soba broth (page 167)

1½ tablespoons katakuriko (potato starch) dissolved in 1½ tablespoons water

2 scallions (about 2 ounces), white parts only, thinly sliced on an angle

Prepare the fresh-frozen udon (see page 175), divide among 4 bowls, and set aside.

Heat the oil in a skillet over medium heat. Add the pork belly and cook, stirring constantly, for about 1 minute, until the pork turns white. Add the onion and cook, stirring constantly, for 2 minutes, until the onions turn translucent. Add the curry powder and cook, stirring constantly, for 10 seconds to toast the curry. Be careful not to burn the curry; scrape the bottom of the skillet. Add the kake soba broth and cook for about 2 minutes. Add the katakuriko mixture and cook, stirring constantly, for about 30 seconds, until the liquid thickens. Reduce the heat to very low to keep warm.

Divide the broth, pork, and onions among the 4 bowls, pouring over the udon. Garnish with the scallions, and serve.

Udon

YAKI UDON

Yaki udon are stir-fried udon noodles, but they aren't cooked crispy. Instead, they're prepared in Japanese seasonings to a springy, tender consistency, along with pork, cabbage, onions, and mushrooms, and simmered until all the ingredients absorb the multitude of delightful flavors in the skillet. Top with dried, shaved bonito flakes, called "dancing bonito" in Japan, because the shavings seem to be swaying to a boogie-woogie beat atop the steaming noodles. You can also substitute the pork with chicken, if you'd like. Use 8 ounces sliced boneless chicken, white or dark meat.

4 bricks (8.8 ounces each) fresh-frozen udon or 4 packages (3.5 ounces each) dried Sanuki udon

1 tablespoon sesame oil

½ medium Spanish onion (about 6 ounces), peeled and thickly sliced

8 ounces fresh pork belly, thinly sliced and cut into bite-size pieces

8 ounces napa cabbage leaves, trimmed and cut into bite-size pieces

4 ounces shiitake mushrooms (about 4 mushrooms), stems removed and sliced

¼ cup sake

2 tablespoons soy sauce

1 teaspoon salt

½ teaspoon ground black pepper

1 cup loosely packed dried, shaved bonito

Prepare the fresh-frozen udon (see page 175), and set aside.

Heat the oil in a large skillet over high heat. Add the onion and pork belly and cook, stirring constantly, for about 1 minute, until the pork turns white. Add the napa cabbage and shiitake and cook, stirring constantly, for 1 minute to soften. Add the sake and simmer for 30 seconds.

Add the soy sauce, stir to combine, and simmer for 30 seconds. Add the noodles, salt, and pepper, and cook, stirring constantly, for about 2 minutes, until the liquid has evaporated.

Divide the noodles, pork, and vegetables among 4 plates. Top each plate with the shaved bonito, and serve immediately.

COLD UDON WITH FRESH TOMATOES

Summer heat? Bring it on! Udon isn't just the province of winter. In this elegant, contemporary dish, cool, chewy noodles are tossed with fresh, delicious tomatoes and fragrant shiso, a Japanese herb, and simply dressed with olive oil and soy sauce. Preparation takes only minutes, with minimal cooking (just boiling the noodles), but this dish is amazing. The perfect meal for summer.

SERVES 4

4 bricks (8.8 ounces each) fresh-frozen udon or 4 packages (3.5 ounces each) dried Sanuki udon

4 ripe beefsteak tomatoes (about 1½ pounds)

¼ cup extra virgin olive oil

¼ cup soy sauce

Pinch pepper

Pinch salt

8 shiso leaves, thinly sliced

Prepare the fresh-frozen udon (see page 175), cool under cold, running water, and drain.

To remove the skin for the tomatoes, prepare an ice bath and set aside. Bring a large pot of water to a boil over high heat. Plunge the tomatoes to the boiling water for 5 seconds, then transfer to the ice bath to cool. The skin will now come off; peel with your fingers.

Transfer the peeled tomatoes to a cutting board and cut each tomato into quarters, then slice the quarters in half horizontally, through the center of each piece, to make

8 pieces. Add the tomatoes, any tomato juice from the cutting board, the olive oil, soy sauce, pepper, and salt to a bowl. Use your hands to knead the tomatoes for about 30 seconds, to bruise them and release their juices, and combine all the flavors in the bowl, creating a fresh, cold tomato sauce. Add the udon and use your hands to mix together with the other ingredients, so the noodles absorb the flavors.

Divide the udon and tomatoes among 4 plates. Garnish with the shiso leaves and serve.

Udon

12 ITAME & CHAHAN

ITAME

Thank the "father of Chinese cooking" in Japan for popularizing these dishes. *Itame* means "stir-fried" or "sautéed," a cooking technique imported from China. A half-century or so ago, a chef named Chin Kenmin opened a Sichuanese Chinese restaurant in Tokyo called Shisen Hanten. The chef tailored his Chinese dishes to Japanese tastes, and they became a sensation. Chef Kenmin began appearing on television to introduce the Japanese to the pleasures of stir-frying, and before long these dishes became standards of home cooks across the country. Fast, flavor-packed, and delicious, these dishes will soon become some of your favorites, too. The recipes that follow include a Chef Kenmin creation as well as other Chinese- and Korean-influenced stir-fries popular in Japan. As in China, a wok is the ideal cooking vessel for these recipes, but a good ol' skillet or even an enameled cast-iron pot (like Le Creuset) works great, too. Finally, always serve steaming white rice with these dishes—and beer, too, if you're so inclined (a crispy Japanese beer and a dish like Reba Nira, page 192, are an inseparable combination).

SAIKORO STEAK

This dish is a favorite of *izakaya* (eating pub) fare, and one that we love. *Saikoro* means "diced," and indeed the steak is cubed, then quickly stir-fried in butter with garlic and scallions, and flavored with soy sauce. It's aromatic, easy to prepare (in two minutes), and incredibly tasty. Don't overcook the steak; you want to serve it medium rare. It's a perfect match to steaming, white rice, and also goes well with refreshing tomato salad (page 80) or creamy potato salad (page 210) or macaroni salad (page 212).

SERVES 4

1 pound sirloin steak, cut into bite-size cubes

Salt and pepper

1 tablespoon butter

1 tablespoon olive oil

4 cloves garlic, peeled and grated

2 scallions (about 2 ounces), trimmed, white and green parts separated, and cut into ¼-inch slices

¼ cup sake

2 tablespoons soy sauce

Season the steak with salt and ground black pepper.

Heat the butter and olive oil in a large skillet over high heat. When the butter has melted and browned, add the steak. Cook, stirring constantly, for about 1 minute, until the steak begins to brown. Add the garlic and white parts of the scallions and cook, stirring constantly, for about 15 seconds. Add the sake and soy sauce, and cook, stirring frequently, for 15 seconds. Add the green parts of the scallions, and cook, stirring frequently, for 30 seconds more. Transfer to a platter and serve immediately.

Itame & Chahan

EBI CHILI

This is Chef Kenmin's tour de force: shrimp stir-fried with chili, which he dished out regularly at his restaurant Shisen Hanten back in the day. Enjoyed now as both *izakaya* (gastro pub) and home fare, this dish is especially popular with kids (of all ages). Full of flavor, the shrimp cooks in just minutes. Chef Kenmin added ketchup to the recipe to appeal to contemporary Japanese tastes and balance the zing of the *tobanjan*. Use a well-seasoned wok or skillet, or a nonstick pan.

SERVES 4

1 tablespoon finely chopped scallion, white parts only

1 teaspoon finely chopped ginger

1 teaspoon finely chopped garlic

1/2 cup torigara stock (page 25)

2 tablespoons sake

1 tablespoon sugar

1/4 cup ketchup

1 teaspoon salt

1/4 teaspoon white pepper

1 pound small shrimp, cleaned, shelled, and deveined

2 tablespoons plus 1/2 teaspoon toasted sesame oil

2 tablespoons katakuriko (potato starch)

2 teaspoons tobanjan (see page 236)

1/2 teaspoon vinegar

4 ounces iceberg lettuce leaves, torn into bite-size pieces

Steamed rice, for serving

Mix together the scallion, ginger, and garlic and set aside.

Mix together the *torigara* stock, 1 tablespoon of the sake, sugar, and ketchup in a bowl and set aside.

Mix together the remaining 1 tablespoon sake, salt, pepper, and shrimp in a large bowl. Add 1/2 teaspoon of the sesame oil and the *katakuriko* and mix together well, making sure to coat all the shrimp.

Heat the remaining 2 tablespoons sesame oil in a large skillet over high heat. Add the shrimp and cook, stirring constantly, for about 30 seconds, until the shrimp begins to turn pink. Add the scallion-ginger mixture and *tobanjan*, and cook, stirring constantly, for about 30 seconds. Add the *torigara* stock mixture and vinegar, and cook, stirring constantly, for about 2 1/2 minutes, until the liquid reduces and thickens into a shiny glaze.

Casually arrange the lettuce pieces on a serving platter and spoon the shrimp over it. Serve immediately, with steaming white rice on the side.

Itame & Chahan

REBA NIRA

This stir-fry of chicken livers and garlic chives became popular in Japan after World War II and is quite similar to the original version you'd find in China. The fragrant garlic chives balance the powerful taste of the liver and add their own appealing flavor. You'll see that we use quite a bit of sesame oil in the recipe; the idea here is to "shock" the liver in the hot oil and seal in its juices. (And besides, livers fried in fragrant sesame oil taste incredible.) A nonstick or well-seasoned cast-iron skillet is the best bet for this dish, because the liver may stick while cooking. If you can't find garlic chives, substitute with scallions or chives; the flavor won't be the same, but the onions work nicely with liver, too.

SERVES 4

1 pound chicken livers, cut into bite-size pieces

1 teaspoon salt

1 tablespoon grated ginger

2 tablespoons sake

1 tablespoon soy sauce

½ cup katakuriko (potato starch), poured onto a plate

¼ cup toasted sesame oil

½ teaspoon tobanjan (see page 236)

1 bunch nira (Japanese garlic chives, about 8 ounces), washed, white parts trimmed, green parts cut into 2-inch pieces

6 ounces soybean sprouts, rinsed well and strained

2 tablespoons oyster sauce

To prepare the liver, rinse the liver in cold, running water and place in a bowl. Add the salt and gently mix together to coat the liver. Rinse the liver again in cold, running water. (This process removes the liver's sliminess.) Lay the liver on a paper towel–lined plate. Pat the liver on top with paper towels to dry.

Mix together the ginger, sake, and soy sauce in a bowl. Add the liver, and gently mix together with your hands until the liver is well coated. Allow the liver to marinate for 10 minutes.

When the liver is ready, dredge each piece, one by one, in the *katakuriko*. Lay the dredged liver on a clean plate.

Heat the sesame oil in a large skillet over high heat. Add the liver pieces to the oil, one by one. Be careful not to splatter the oil. When all the liver is in the skillet, move the skillet to swirl the oil around the pan to coat the liver. Cook for about 30 seconds, then turn the liver, one by one, to cook the other side. Cook for 30 seconds more. Carefully remove the skillet from the heat, and pour off about half of the oil in the skillet. Return the skillet to the heat. Add the *tobanjan*, *nira*, and bean sprouts. Cook, stirring frequently, for about 1 minute, until the chives and spouts soften. Add the oyster sauce and cook, stirring frequently, for 1 minute more. Transfer to a platter and serve immediately.

TON SHOGA-YAKI

SERVES 4

In this dish, also inspired by Chinese cooking, we stir-fry pork with ginger. Not only does ginger add wonderful flavor but it also tempers the "porkiness" of pork (Japanese cooking is all about balancing flavors). This fast-cooking dish is a summertime favorite in Japan; the pork and ginger help revive you on a steamy hot day.

¼ cup soy sauce

2 tablespoons sake

2 tablespoons sugar

2 teaspoons grated ginger

½ teaspoon salt

½ teaspoon ground black pepper

1 pound shaved pork shoulder (available at Asian markets, or ask your butcher)

2 tablespoons toasted sesame oil

½ large Spanish onion (about 8 ounces), peeled and thinly sliced

4 ounces iceberg lettuce leaves, torn into bite-size pieces

Steamed rice, for serving

Mix together the soy sauce, sake, sugar, ginger, salt, and black pepper in a large bowl. Add the pork and use your hands to mix together well, so the meat is evenly coated.

Heat the sesame oil in a large skillet over high heat. Add the onion and cook, stirring constantly, for about 2 minutes, until the onions turn translucent. Add the pork and cook, stirring constantly, for about 4 minutes, until the meat has cooked through. Break apart the pork slices as you stir, so you have small pieces of meat in the dish.

Casually arrange the lettuce pieces on a serving platter and spoon the pork over it. Serve immediately, with steaming white rice on the side.

MOTTSU MISO ITAME

Mottsu is the Japanese word for "offal." Cooked with miso it makes a delicious, savory stew. Inexpensive to prepare, it became popular with the rickshaw pullers who once plied Tokyo's streets. You can still find huge pots of mottsu bubbling on outdoor burners on the side streets of the old neighborhoods, just like back in the day. In this recipe, we use tripe, which will cook down by half as you prepare it. When you're ready to stir-fry, make sure your skillet or wok is well seasoned or nonstick, or the tripe may stick while cooking.

SERVES 4

2 pounds tripe, rinsed and cut into bite-size pieces

3 tablespoons red miso (see page 234)

2 tablespoons sake

1 tablespoon mirin

2 teaspoons tobanjan (see page 236)

2 tablespoons toasted sesame oil

½ medium Spanish onion (about 6 ounces), peeled and coarsely chopped

2 cloves garlic, peeled and thinly sliced

2 scallions (about 2 ounces), trimmed and coarsely chopped

To prepare the tripe, place in a large saucepan, cover with water, and bring to a boil over high heat. Remove the tripe and discard the water. Add the tripe back to the saucepan, cover with water again, and bring to a boil over high heat. Reduce the heat to low and simmer the tripe, uncovered, for 2 hours, to make it tender. Strain the tripe, rinse under cold water, and set aside.

Combine the miso, sake, mirin, and *tobanjan* in a bowl and set aside.

Heat the sesame oil in a large skillet over high heat. Add the tripe, and cook, stirring constantly, for about 5 minutes, until browned. Be careful that the tripe doesn't stick to the bottom of the skillet. Add the onion and garlic, and cook, stirring constantly, for 1 minute more. Add the miso mixture, and cook, stirring constantly, for 30 seconds. Add the scallions and cook, stirring constantly, for 30 seconds, until they turn bright green. Transfer to a platter and serve immediately.

JAPANESE-STYLE BULGOGI

Bulgogi is a classic of Korean cooking, where meat and vegetables are marinated in soy sauce, sesame oil, garlic, and other ingredients, and then grilled. In the Japanese adaptation, the meat and vegetables are also marinated, but instead of grilling, they're stir-fried. Also, the Japanese recipe calls for traditional seasonings like sake and mirin, to add umami flavor to the marinade. Both versions of this dish, though, share one key thing: they both taste amazing! When cooking this recipe, be sure to evaporate almost all of the liquid out of the skillet or wok. You want the dish dry, not soupy. But be careful not to burn it as you cook it down.

SERVES 4

¼ cup soy sauce

¼ cup sake

2 tablespoons mirin

2 teaspoons tobanjan (see page 236)

1 teaspoon salt

½ teaspoon ground black pepper

1 tablespoon sugar

2 teaspoons grated garlic

¼ cup toasted sesame oil

1 pound shaved beef (look for shabu-shabu beef at Asian markets or ask your butcher), cut into bite-size pieces

½ large Spanish onion (about 8 ounces), peeled and thinly sliced

1 medium carrot (about 4 ounces), peeled and cut into matchsticks

1 small green bell pepper (about 6 ounces), cored and cut into matchsticks

3 ounces shiitake mushrooms, stemmed and thinly sliced

2 teaspoons sesame seed

Steamed rice, for serving

Mix together the soy sauce, sake, mirin, *tobanjan*, salt, black pepper, sugar, garlic, and 2 tablespoons of the sesame oil in a large bowl. Add the beef, and use your hands to mix together well, so the meat is evenly coated. Add the onion, carrot, bell pepper, and shiitake, and mix together well.

Heat the remaining 2 tablespoons sesame oil in a large skillet over high heat. Add the beef, vegetables, and marinade. Cook, stirring constantly, for about 7 minutes, or until the liquid in the skillet has almost completely evaporated and the ingredients begin caramelizing. Be careful not to burn. Break apart the meat as you stir.

Transfer the meat and vegetables to a serving platter, garnish with the sesame seed, and serve with steaming white rice on the side.

GENGHIS KHAN

A Japanese dish named in honor of the legendary Mongolian warlord? The connection is sheep, which were imported in the early twentieth century to the northern island of Hokkaido and raised for wool. Eventually, locals started eating mutton and lamb, just like they do in Mongolia, and some creative someone came up with an unforgettable name for the dish. By 1936, its popularity had spread and the first Genghis Khan restaurant opened up in Tokyo. If you love lamb as much as we do, try this delicious stir-fry packed with flavor. The apple in the recipe adds a subtle layer of underlying sweetness, just lovely.

SERVES 4

1 large apple (about 7 ounces), peeled, cored, and coarsely chopped

½ medium Spanish onion (about 6 ounces), peeled and coarsely chopped

¾ ounce ginger (about 1-inch piece) peeled and coarsely chopped

1 tablespoon coarsely chopped garlic

¼ cup sake

1 tablespoon soy sauce

2 teaspoons red miso (see page 234)

1 pound lamb shoulder, cut into bite-size strips

½ teaspoon salt

¼ teaspoon pepper

2 tablespoons toasted sesame oil

8 ounces green cabbage, cored and cut into bite-size pieces

6 ounces soybean sprouts, rinsed and drained

2 tablespoons oyster sauce

Add the apple, onion, ginger, garlic, sake, soy sauce, and red miso to the work bowl of a blender. Pulse for about 2 minutes, until they combine into a smooth sauce.

Season the lamb with salt and ground black pepper.

Heat the sesame oil in a large skillet over high heat. Add the lamb and cook, stirring constantly, for about 2 minutes, until the lamb begins to brown. Add the cabbage and bean sprouts and cook, stirring constantly, for 2 minutes more. Add the apple-sake sauce and cook, stirring constantly, for 2 minutes, until the liquid cooks down. Add the oyster sauce and cook, stirring frequently, for 2 minutes. Transfer to a platter and serve immediately.

CHAHAN

Chahan is another stir-fried culinary import from China—fried rice, Japanese style. It's believed to have first turned up at the port city of Kobe in the 1860s with the arrival of Chinese immigrants. With chahan, you use cooked rice to prepare the dish, like in China (as opposed to using raw grains for European rice dishes like risotto or paella). Chahan is a terrific method to deliciously dispense with leftover rice, whether at a restaurant or at home. (If you don't use a rice cooker that keeps leftover rice warm, like in Japan, stick cold rice in the microwave for a few seconds to warm it up.)

Keep a few things in mind when cooking this dish. Use high heat and cook quickly so the rice doesn't stick to the pan. So make sure you preheat your pan thoroughly before cooking. In fact, fried rice in China harks back to the Song Dynasty (960–1279), a time when Chinese began cooking in iron pots over coal fires, and were first able to get their pots hot enough for this dish. But you don't need a Song Dynasty iron pot; a wok, a nonstick pan, or an enameled cast-iron pot like Le Creuset works great.

For best results, use warm rice and shake your wok or pot while you fry the rice, to move ingredients around. The consistency you want is rice that's dry and crumbly, not wet. So be patient and attentive as you reduce out the liquid while you cook, so you don't burn the rice. Oh, and cooking this dish always makes a mess, with rice flying all over the place. But, hey, that's okay. (At least in our kitchens.) Finally, Japanese eat chahan with a spoon, not chopsticks—a nod to China, perhaps, where they eat fried rice the same way.

CLASSIC PORK CHAHAN

SERVES 4

2 tablespoons plus 1 teaspoon toasted sesame oil

4 eggs, beaten

4 ounces fresh pork belly, thinly sliced and cut into ½-inch cubes

2 scallions (about 2 ounces), trimmed and coarsely chopped

1 teaspoon finely chopped garlic

4 cups cooked rice, warm, clumps broken up

1 teaspoon salt

1 teaspoon pepper

1 tablespoon oyster sauce

1 tablespoon soy sauce

This is the classic version of chahan, cooked with pork. But you can adapt this basic recipe to a bunch of other ingredients. We list some suggestions in the variations below. In Japan, chahan is often eaten with *beni shoga* as a condiment, *beni shoga* being red-pickled ginger, tangy and bright. If you want to make your chahan extra pretty, dish the fried rice into a rice bowl and then use the bowl as a mold—flip it upside down on a plate and then remove, so the rice remaining is shaped like a perfect dome. A nice touch. Chahan is perfect served as the main event or as a side dish.

Heat 1 teaspoon of the sesame oil in a wok over high heat. Add the eggs and gently scramble until set, about 10 seconds. Remove the eggs and set aside.

Heat 1 tablespoon of the sesame oil in the wok over high heat. Add the pork, and cook for 1 minute, stirring constantly, until the pork turns white. Add the scallions and garlic, and cook, stirring constantly, for 30 seconds more, until they wilt and give off an oniony aroma. Add the cooked eggs, and cook, stirring constantly, for 15 seconds. Add the rice and cook for 1 minute, stirring constantly, to incorporate it with the pork, egg, and scallions. Break up any remaining clumps of rice.

Sprinkle with the salt and pepper and cook, stirring constantly, for 30 seconds. Add the oyster sauce and soy sauce, and cook, stirring constantly, for 1 minute. Add the remaining 1 tablespoon sesame oil and cook, stirring constantly, for 1 minute. Serve immediately.

Variations You can substitute the pork belly with 4 ounces of crabmeat, shrimp, bacon, *chashu* (page 9), boneless dark-meat chicken, or ground beef. Cut the shrimp, bacon, *chashu*, or chicken into bite-size pieces. For a vegetarian version, you can substitute 2 tablespoons of thinly sliced garlic for the pork belly.

KANI ANKAKE (CRAB FRIED RICE)

With this dish, the fried rice is cooked very simply, with just eggs and scallions. The mojo here comes in the form of the *ankake*, which is a sauce thickened with potato starch, in this case, one made with ginger-infused crabmeat. Glorious. To eat, spoon up some *ankake* with the fried rice.

SERVES 4

2 tablespoons plus 1 teaspoon toasted sesame oil

4 eggs, beaten

2 scallions (about 2 ounces), trimmed and chopped

4 cups cooked rice, warm, clumps broken up

2 tablespoons soy sauce

1 teaspoon salt

Pinch ground black pepper

ankake

8 ounces crabmeat (canned is fine, about 1 cup)

1 cup torigara stock (page 25)

4 ounces iceberg lettuce leaves, cut into bite-size pieces

1 (½-inch) piece ginger (about 0.3 ounce), peeled and julienned

1 teaspoon salt

¼ teaspoon ground black pepper

2 teaspoons katakuriko (potato starch) dissolved in 2 tablespoons water

Heat 1 teaspoon of the sesame oil in a wok over high heat. Add the eggs and gently scramble until set, about 10 seconds. Remove the eggs and set aside.

Heat 1 tablespoon of the sesame oil in a wok over high heat. Add the scallions and cook, stirring constantly, for about 30 seconds, until they give off an oniony smell. Add the rice, and cook, stirring constantly, for 30 seconds more. Add the soy sauce, salt, pepper, and cooked eggs. Cook, stirring constantly, for 30 seconds. Add the remaining 1 tablespoon sesame oil, and cook, stirring constantly, for 10 more seconds. Turn off the heat.

Arrange 4 plates on a work surface, and ready 4 small bowls to serve as molds (rice bowls are ideal). Spoon one-fourth of the cooked rice into a bowl, then quickly flip the bowl over, and rest it on top of the plate rice side down. Do not remove the bowl for now; it will keep the rice warm. Repeat with the remaining 3 bowls. Set aside.

To prepare the *ankake*, add the crab, *torigara* stock, lettuce, ginger, salt, and pepper to a saucepan and bring to a boil over heat. Reduce the heat to medium and simmer for about 2 minutes, mixing occasionally. Add the *katakuriko* mixture, and cook, stirring constantly, for about 15 seconds. Turn off the heat.

Unmold the rice by removing the bowls covering it. Pour about one-fourth of the *ankake* either alongside each serving of rice or over it, as you desire. Serve immediately.

CHICKEN CURRY CHAHAN

Japan can't seem to get enough of curry. Here we have a "dry curry" fried rice, an incredibly popular home-cooked dish. The curry flavor works so nicely, melding with bits of chicken and root vegetables, and, of course, the rice. We've seen Japanese home cooks also add raisins to this dish, which gives it another interesting, sweet flavor layer. Feel free to reduce the amount of curry powder, if you like your food less hot. Mold the cooked rice in a bowl as we explain on page 201 if you want to gussy up your presentation. Finally, pay close attention when you cook this rice, because the curry can burn easily.

SERVES 4

1 tablespoon butter

1 tablespoon olive oil

2 chicken legs (about 8 ounces), skinned, boned, and cut into bite-size pieces

¼ large Spanish onion (about 4 ounces), peeled and chopped

¾ medium carrot (about 3 ounces), peeled and chopped

1 stalk celery (about 2 ounces), trimmed and chopped

2 cloves garlic, thinly sliced

3 tablespoons curry powder

¼ cup sake

4 cups cooked rice, warm, clumps broken up

1 tablespoon soy sauce

1 tablespoon Worcestershire sauce

1 teaspoon salt

½ teaspoon ground black pepper

1 tablespoon finely chopped parsley

Heat the butter and olive oil in a wok over high heat. When the butter has melted, add the chicken and cook, stirring constantly, for 2 minutes, until the chicken turns white. Add the onion, carrot, celery, and garlic, and cook, stirring constantly, for 2 minutes, until the vegetables soften. Add the curry powder and cook, stirring constantly, for 30 seconds, to toast the curry. Add the sake and cook, stirring constantly, for 30 seconds. Add the rice and cook, stirring constantly, for 1 minute. Break up any remaining clumps of rice, and be sure to scrape the bottom of the wok because the curry burns easily. Add the soy sauce, Worcestershire sauce, salt, and pepper and cook for 30 seconds more, stirring constantly. Turn off the heat.

Divide the rice among 4 plates and garnish with the parsley. Serve immediately.

EBI PILAF

Japanese pilaf is a take on the original pilaf, which is served from the Indian subcontinent to Europe. The major difference is that with the Japanese version you use cooked rice rather than raw rice. Very simple but satisfying, ebi pilaf works great as a side dish.

SERVES 4

2 tablespoons butter

¼ large Spanish onion (about 4 ounces), peeled and coarsely chopped

¾ medium carrot (about 3 ounces), peeled and diced

8 ounces small shrimp, cleaned, peeled, and deveined

1 small green bell pepper (about 6 ounces), cored and diced

¼ cup torigara stock (page 25)

1 teaspoon salt

½ teaspoon pepper

4 cups cooked rice, warm, clumps broken up

Melt the butter in a wok over high heat. Add the onion and carrot and cook, stirring constantly, for about 1 minute, until the vegetables soften. Add the shrimp and cook, stirring constantly, for about 1 minute. Add the bell pepper and cook, stirring constantly, for 30 seconds. Add the *torigara* stock and cook for 30 seconds. Add the salt, pepper, and rice and cook, stirring constantly, for about 1 minute until most of the liquid has evaporated and the rice has the dry consistency of chahan (page 198). Serve immediately.

13 YOSHOKU

YOSHOKU

Yoshoku means "Western-style cooking," and, indeed, the dishes in this chapter are all direct adaptations of European and American favorites. As we describe in the book's introduction, when Westerners began streaming into Japan in the mid-1800s, they brought with them their own grub, of course. And before long, this cooking began to influence Japanese cuisine in general across the country. Fancy hotels in port towns like Yokohama contributed to the spread of Western-influenced cuisine by hiring foreign cooks and chefs (see Doria, page 214), who shared their knowledge with their Japanese counterparts. Furthermore, Japanese military cooks also learned about Western-style cooking from foreign soldiers they encountered.

All this led to a slew of Western dishes being adapted, transformed, and evolved into a singular Japanese culinary style, one that spread from restaurants to homes across the country. And while the dishes are inspired by Western cuisine, one thing has remained uniquely Japanese: all the dishes in this chapter, save for the gratins and pasta for obvious reasons, are meant to be served with steaming white rice on the side—it's the rice that makes them truly yoshoku.

WHITE SAUCE

This sauce has its roots in classic French béchamel sauce, and serves as the basis of the Ebi Gratin and Doria recipes that follow.

4 tablespoons butter

½ cup flour

1 quart milk, warmed in saucepan or microwave (don't boil)

Melt the butter in a saucepan over low heat. Prepare a roux by gradually adding the flour to the melted butter, while whisking constantly. When you've added all the flour, cook and whisk constantly for about 2 minutes. The flour will first bind to the butter, then the mixture will break apart, and finally, it will firm up and look like large blonde crumbs when it's ready. Be careful not to burn or color the roux; you want it to turn out blonde-colored rather than brown-colored.

Gradually add the milk to the roux, while whisking constantly. Add about one-fourth of the milk every 1 minute, cooking and whisking constantly, to slowly incorporate the milk into the roux. The sauce will gradually become smooth. Once you've added all the milk, cook the sauce for about 2 minutes, whisking constantly, to thicken it. Be careful not to burn; be sure to scrape the bottom of the pan as you whisk. The sauce will become smooth and velvety with the consistency of heavy cream, and little bubbles will appear on the surface. Remove the sauce from the heat and allow it to cool.

EBI GRATIN

While the ingredients don't seem particularly Japanese in this gratin, except maybe the shrimp (*ebi* in Japanese), this dish has become much beloved in Japan, like Doria (page 214). But here we use actual macaroni rather than rice—so consider ebi gratin the true Japanese mac 'n' cheese. Velvety, smooth, and cheesy, with a beautifully crispy crust, it's a delight. And don't forget, ebi gratin makes a great side dish.

SERVES 4

8 ounces elbow macaroni

2 tablespoons butter

½ medium Spanish onion (about 6 ounces), peeled and coarsely chopped

8 ounces small shrimp, cleaned, peeled, and deveined

¼ cup white wine

1½ teaspoons salt

½ teaspoon pepper

3 cups white sauce (page 207)

4 ounces Gruyère cheese, coarsely grated

4 ounces Parmesan cheese, coarsely grated

Cook the macaroni according to package instructions. Strain and cool the noodles under cold, running water. Set aside.

Preheat an oven broiler.

Melt 1 tablespoon of the butter in a large saucepan over medium heat. Add the onion and cook, stirring constantly, for about 1 minute to soften. Add the shrimp and cook, stirring constantly, for about 2 minutes, until they turn pink. Add the white wine, salt, pepper, and white sauce. Reduce the heat to low and cook, stirring constantly, for 30 seconds to combine all the ingredients. Add the macaroni and cook, stirring constantly, for 1 minute to thoroughly combine. Remove the saucepan from the heat and set aside.

Grease a large ceramic or glass baking dish with the remaining 1 tablespoon butter. Transfer the noodle mixture to the baking dish and spread it out evenly. Sprinkle the Gruyère and Parmesan on top. Place the baking dish under the broiler and broil for 3 to 4 minutes, until the cheese melts and forms a browned and crispy crust. Serve immediately.

POTATO SALADA

SERVES 4

There are a couple of theories about the origins of Japanese potato salad, but the one we're going with is that it was inspired by Russian-style potato salad. Sounds plausible. Potato salad is taken so seriously in Japan that a leading food magazine once gathered a panel of experts to determine the perfect ratio of mayo to spuds, depending on the particular potato variety. Whoa. Well, the fact is that there are tons of potato salad variations in Japan. The one below is Tadashi's favorite, which is straightforward and delicious. You'll see that he lightly cures the vegetables in salt, which turns them bright-colored and even more flavorful. This salad works great as a side to any of the dishes in this chapter.

2 medium Idaho potatoes (about 1 pound), peeled and coarsely chopped

1 tablespoon plus 1½ teaspoon salt

4 ounces cucumber, thinly sliced (if using Japanese or Persian cucumbers, leave the skin on; otherwise, peel and remove seeds)

½ medium carrot (about 2 ounces), peeled, thinly sliced

¼ medium Spanish onion (about 3 ounces), peeled and thinly sliced

½ cup water

1 tablespoon vinegar

¼ cup Kewpie mayonnaise

Pinch ground black pepper

To cook the potatoes, fill a saucepan large enough to cover the potatoes with water and add 1 tablespoon of the salt. Place over high heat and bring to a boil. Reduce the heat to medium, and cook the potatoes for about 10 minutes, or until a skewer goes through them easily. Drain and coarsely mash the potatoes, so small chunks are still visible. Set aside and allow the potatoes to come to room temperature.

Add the cucumber, carrot, onion, and 1 teaspoon of the salt to a bowl. Use your hands to mix the ingredients, making sure they're coated well with the salt. Allow the vegetables to cure for 5 minutes. Add the water and swirl the ingredients in the water to remove the salt. Squeeze the cured vegetables tightly with your hands to expel the liquid.

Add the vegetables and the potatoes to a large bowl and mix together well. Add the vinegar and mix to combine. Add the mayonnaise, pepper, and the remaining ½ teaspoon salt. Mix together well, until the salad is smooth, and serve.

Variations You can also add 2 hard-boiled eggs, for extra richness and flavor. Mash the eggs and add them along with the potatoes and cured vegetables.

You can also riff on this recipe in a bunch of ways, to wit: Add 1 ounce of mentaiko, spicy marinated pollock roe. Or add ¼ cup cooked hijiki. Or add 2 tablespoons of chopped shiso leaves, or 1 tablespoon of curry powder, or 2 teaspoons of *karashi* mustard, or 1 teaspoon of *shichimi togarashi*, or 2 teaspoons of wasabi, or 1 teaspoon of red *yuzu kosho*.

MACARONI SALADA

A French missionary built the first macaroni factory in Japan in 1883. Back then, pasta was considered fancy grub and was served at tony restaurants and luxury hotels. But with the American influence post–World War II, it gained popularity as an everyday food—hey, it's just macaroni, after all. As with our potato salad (page 210), this is a straight-forward, easy, and delicious recipe (pictured on page 81). But as with our potato salad, too, you can gussy it up by adding 2 tablespoons of chopped shiso leaves, or 1 tablespoon of curry powder, or 2 teaspoons of *karashi* mustard, or 1 teaspoon of *shichimi togarashi*, or 2 teaspoons of wasabi, or 1 teaspoon of red *yuzu kosho*. All these variations are terrific. Also, like potato salad, macaroni salad is a perfect side for yoshoku dishes.

SERVES 4

4 ounces elbow macaroni

3 ounces cucumber, julienned (if using Japanese or Persian cucumbers, leave the skin on; otherwise, peel and remove seeds)

1/2 medium carrot (about 2 ounces), peeled and julienned

1 teaspoon salt

1/2 cup water

3 ounces sliced ham, cut into strips

1 teaspoon vinegar

1/4 cup Kewpie mayonnaise

Pinch ground black pepper

Cook the macaroni according to package instructions. Strain and cool the noodles under cold, running water. Set aside.

Add the cucumber, carrot, and 1/2 teaspoon of the salt to a bowl. Use your hands to mix the ingredients, making sure they're coated well with the salt. Allow the vegetables to cure for 5 minutes. Add the water and swirl the ingredients in the water to remove the salt. Squeeze the cured vegetables tightly with your hands to expel the liquid.

Add the vegetables, macaroni, and the ham to a large bowl and mix together well. Add the vinegar and mix to combine. Add the mayonnaise, pepper, and remaining 1/2 teaspoon salt. Mix together well, and serve.

LETTUCE WITH GINGER-CARROT DRESSING

The gingery dressing here is so tangy and refreshing, you might want to double the batch and keep some handy. (It will keep for 2 weeks in the refrigerator.) In addition to lettuce (as pictured on page 81), you can add cucumber, red radish, or tomatoes to this salad. Also, you can substitute the iceberg lettuce with romaine or green cabbage.

2 medium carrots (about 8 ounces), peeled, trimmed and roughly chopped

1/2 medium Spanish onion (about 6 ounces), roughly chopped

1/2 tablespoon finely chopped ginger

1/2 cup Japanese rice vinegar

1/4 cup soy sauce

1 cup vegetable oil

1 tablespoon sugar

1/2 teaspoon salt

1 head (about 1 pound) iceberg lettuce, trimmed and cut into bite-sized pieces

Place the carrots, onion, ginger, vinegar, soy sauce, oil, sugar, and salt in the work bowl of a blender. Pulse for about 1 minute, until the ingredients become a smooth dressing. (Depending on the size of your blender, you might need to do this in batches.)

Arrange the lettuce on 4 plates, drizzle 1/4 of the dressing over each plate, and serve.

DORIA

This is a dish named after a real-life count called Doria, who hailed from Genoa, Italy. Why? Nobody knows. What we do know is that in 1927, a Swiss chef named Saly Weil was working at the Hotel New Grand in Yokahama, when a guest with a sensitive stomach asked for something comforting. Chef Weil obliged with this gratin-style dish. His Japanese kitchen apprentices loved this dish so much that when they finally became chefs in their own right, they served it at their own restaurants and hotels, and Doria eventually became an enduring comfort food standard, to this very day. Use leftover rice if you have it; it's perfect for this dish.

SERVES 4

2 tablespoons butter

1/2 medium Spanish onion (about 6 ounces), peeled and coarsely chopped

8 ounces boneless chicken breast, cut into 1/2-inch cubes

6 ounces white button mushrooms, trimmed and thinly sliced

1 1/2 teaspoons salt

1/2 teaspoon pepper

1/4 cup white wine

3 cups white sauce (page 207)

4 cups cooked white rice

4 ounces Gruyère cheese, coarsely grated

4 ounces Parmesan cheese, coarsely grated

Preheat an oven broiler.

Melt 1 tablespoon of the butter in a large saucepan over medium heat. Add the onion and cook, stirring constantly, for about 1 minute to soften. Add the chicken and cook, stirring constantly, for about 2 minutes until it turns white. Add the mushrooms and cook, stirring constantly, for about 1 minute. Add the salt, pepper, wine, and white sauce. Reduce the heat to low and cook, stirring constantly, for 30 seconds to combine all the ingredients. Add the rice and cook, stirring constantly, for about 1 minute, until the rice absorbs the sauce and resembles risotto. Remove the saucepan from the heat and set aside.

Grease a large ceramic or glass baking dish with the remaining 1 tablespoon butter. Transfer the rice mixture to the baking dish and spread it out evenly. Sprinkle the Gruyère and Parmesan on top. Place the baking dish under the broiler and broil for 3 to 4 minutes, until the cheese melts and forms a browned and crispy crust. Serve immediately.

OMU RICE

Remember our friends at Rengatei, that inventive Western-style restaurant in Tokyo that bequeathed to the world tonkatsu (page 60), kaki furai (page 78), and other dishes that became Japanese comfort classics? Well, it seems that a customer there, sometime around 1900, spied the staff going to town on curious omelets during *makanai* (staff meal), which were not on the regular menu. The customer asked for what the cooks were eating (always a good move), and was served the same dish. Other customers then asked for it, and on and on, and before long the dish, *omu raisu* (a Japanglish contraction of "omelet" and "rice"), became enduringly popular across Japan.

The omelet is stuffed with fried rice, usually cooked with chicken, and always flavored with ketchup. It might seem kinda odd at first to the American eye—but kinda irresistible, too, believe us. Make the omelets one at a time. Shrimp also works great instead of the chicken. And get creative with the ketchup garnish at the end, if you'd like. We opted for a straight line (yawn—but easy), but if you've got a deft hand, use the ketchup to draw a heart, a Hello Kitty, or whatever!

SERVES 4

½ cup torigara stock (page 25)

½ cup ketchup

2 tablespoons butter

8 ounces boneless chicken breast, skinned and cut into ½-inch cubes

¼ large Spanish onion (about 4 ounces), peeled and coarsely chopped

¾ medium carrot (about 3 ounces), peeled and coarsely chopped

½ teaspoon salt

½ teaspoon ground black pepper

4 cups cooked rice, warm, clumps broken up

½ cup cooked peas

omelets

8 eggs

4 teaspoons milk

Salt

Ground black pepper

4 teaspoons butter

4 tablespoons ketchup

Whisk together the torigara stock and ketchup and set aside.

Melt the butter in a wok over high heat. Add the chicken and cook for 1 minute, stirring constantly, until the chicken turns white. Add the onion and carrot and cook for 1 minute. Add the torigara and ketchup mixture, salt, and pepper and simmer for about 3 minutes, until most of the liquid has evaporated and the ingredients are coated with a thick ketchup sauce. Stir frequently; the sugars in the ketchup can burn. Add the rice and cook, stirring constantly, for about 2 minutes. Break up any remaining clumps of rice. Add the peas and cook, stirring constantly, for about 30 seconds more. Set aside.

To prepare one omelet at a time, beat 2 of the eggs with 1 teaspoon of the milk and pinches of salt and pepper.

Melt 1 teaspoon of the butter in a small skillet over medium heat. Pour in the beaten egg. Spread the egg in the pan to make a thin omelet. Break any air bubbles that might form. Cook for about 1 minute, until the egg sets (don't flip). Turn off

continued >

Yoshoku

the heat. Spoon about one-fourth of the rice mixture over one half of the omelet. Carefully tilt the skillet over while sliding the egg onto a plate, so the rice is sandwiched between halves of the omelet. Pour 1 tablespoon of the ketchup over the omelet, in a straight line. Serve immediately.

Repeat this process to make the remaining 3 omelets.

YOSHOKU STEAK

This is a Western-style hunk of prime beef, but with a Japanese flair. The steak is topped with onions that have been reduced and caramelized with Japanese seasonings and cut with rice vinegar. So incredibly mouthwatering! We adapted this steak from the original recipe of the Imperial Hotel in Tokyo, one of Tokyo's oldest and classiest hotels. In 1936, a Russian opera star named Feodor Chaliapin was a guest there, and requested a tender steak. The chef complied, with this dish. The bass virtuoso was delighted, and so apparently, was the hotel, which promptly put it on the menu. Eat this steak with a knife and fork; serve with rice and steamed or sautéed vegetables on the side. Besides sirloin, you can use rib eye, tenderloin, or filet mignon.

SERVES 4

4 sirloin steaks (about 2 pounds total)

Salt

Ground black pepper

3 tablespoons butter

1 medium Spanish onion (about 12 ounces), peeled and finely chopped

2 cloves garlic, finely chopped

¼ cup mirin

¼ cup soy sauce

1 teaspoon rice vinegar

1 tablespoon vegetable oil

2 teaspoons chopped parsley

To tenderize the steaks, lay them flat on a cutting board. Tap the steaks with the back edge of a kitchen knife (the edge opposite the blade) to dig notches into the meat. Turn the knife so the flat side is facing the fillets. Pound the meat with the knife's flat side about 6 to 8 times on each side of the steak to flatten the meat. Season both sides of the meat with salt and pepper.

Melt 2 tablespoons of the butter in a skillet over low heat. Add the onion and garlic and cook, stirring frequently, for about 8 minutes, until the onions are translucent and caramelized and have developed their sweetness. Increase the heat to medium. Add the mirin and soy sauce and cook, stirring constantly, for about 1 minute, to cook down the liquid. Add the vinegar and cook, stirring constantly, for 30 seconds more. Transfer to a bowl and set aside.

Melt the remaining 1 tablespoon butter and the oil in a large skillet over medium-high heat. When the butter has melted and started to brown, cook the steaks in batches. Lay the steaks in the skillet, and cook for about 4 minutes, turning once (for medium rare). Transfer the steaks to a cutting board and allow them to rest for 1 minute before serving.

Return the skillet to medium-high heat. Add the onions and cook, stirring constantly, for about 10 seconds, so the onions absorb the steaks juices remaining in the skillet.

Top the steaks with the onion mixture, garnish with the parsley, and serve immediately.

HAMBURG

A hamburger without the "er"—what shakes? Forget the bun, forget the sliced onion, the bacon, the Cheddar, the grilled mushrooms, etc., etc. What we're talking here is the Japanese version, and it's fantastic. Yes, hamburg was influenced by American hamburgers and became popular when the Yanks administered Japan after World War II. But this particular patty is served on a plate with a tangy ketchup-based sauce on top, sans bun. And it's made with both ground beef and ground pork, panko crumbs, and—surprise—milk. It's always cooked well done (because of the pork). And guess what? It's incredibly juicy, thanks to the milk and panko, and incredibly tasty, thanks to the mixture of meat and that amazing reduction sauce. Terrific with potato salad (page 210), sliced tomatoes, or sautéed or steamed vegetables. Also, steamed white rice on the side is a must.

SERVES 4

2 tablespoons butter

½ medium Spanish onion (about 6 ounces), peeled and finely chopped

1 clove garlic, finely chopped

½ cup panko crumbs (page 61)

½ cup milk

8 ounces ground pork

8 ounces ground beef

½ teaspoon salt

1 teaspoon soy sauce

1 egg

1 tablespoon vegetable oil, plus more for hands

¼ cup sake

¼ cup Worcester sauce

½ cup ketchup

4 sprigs parsley (optional)

Melt 1 tablespoon of the butter in a skillet over medium-low heat. Add the onion and garlic and cook, stirring constantly, for about 5 minutes, until the onions become translucent and soft and release their sweetness. Make sure not to burn the onions while you cook. Remove the skillet from the heat and allow the onions to cool to room temperature.

Mix together the panko crumbs and milk in a bowl, and allow the mixture to sit for at least 5 minutes, for the panko to completely absorb the milk.

Add the pork, beef, salt, soy sauce, egg, cooked onions, and panko and milk mixture to a large bowl. Use your hands to mix the ingredients together for at least 2 minutes. Press the ingredients with your hands and squeeze them through your fingers; you want the meat mixture to become well blended and slightly sticky so it holds together while cooking.

Divide the meat mixture into 4 equal parts. Lightly dab your hands with oil, so the meat doesn't stick to them. Using your palms, gently form each part into a patty about 1 inch thick. Press down to make a slight indentation in the center of each patty, which prevents it from puffing up as it cooks.

Heat the remaining 1 tablespoon butter and remaining 1 tablespoon oil in a large skillet over medium heat. When the butter melts, lay the patties in the skillet. Cook for about 12 minutes, flipping once, until the patty is cooked through. Check the patty by poking it with a skewer; if the juices run clear, it's done. Transfer the patties to 4 plates, and garnish with the parsley.

continued >

Keep the skillet over the heat. Add the sake and swirl the liquid for about 20 seconds, scraping the bottom of the skillet to deglaze it. Add the Worcestershire sauce and ketchup and cook, stirring constantly, for about 1 minute to create a sauce.

Pour the sauce over the hamburg and serve immediately.

PORK SAUTÉ

Like Yoshoku Steak (page 219), this dish is Western-style hunk of meat meets savory Japanese flavors. But in this case, we pan-sauté boneless pork loin fillets with sake, soy sauce, and butter. The combo of soy sauce and butter is particularly sensational. Try sautéing anything with soy sauce and butter—steaks, green beans, mushrooms, chicken breast, or, yes, pork loin—it'll blow your mind. Like Yoshoku Steak, this dish is eaten in Japan with a fork and knife; serve with rice and steamed or sautéed vegetables on the side.

SERVES 4

4 boneless pork loin fillets (about 2 pounds)
Salt
Ground black pepper
5 tablespoons butter
1 tablespoon oil
¼ cup sake
¼ cup lemon juice
¼ soy sauce

To tenderize the pork fillets, lay them flat on a cutting board. Tap the fillets with the back edge of a kitchen knife (the edge opposite the blade) to dig notches into the meat. Turn the knife so the flat side is facing the fillets. Pound the meat with the knife's flat side about 6 to 8 times on each side of the pork to flatten the meat to about 1/2 inch thick. Season both sides of the pork with salt and pepper.

Heat 1 tablespoon of the butter and the oil in a skillet over medium-high heat. When the butter has turned brown, add the pork fillets. Cook for about 6 minutes total, to cook through the pork. Start by cooking on one side for 2 minutes. Turn and cook for 3 minutes on the other side.

Turn again, and cook for 1 minute more. Transfer the fillets to a cutting board and allow them to rest for 20 seconds. Cut the pork into slices and arrange on 4 plates.

Keep the skillet over the heat. Add the sake and swirl the liquid for about 20 seconds, scraping the bottom of the skillet to deglaze it. Add the lemon juice and soy sauce, and cook, stirring constantly, for about 20 seconds. Add the remaining 4 tablespoons butter and cook, stirring constantly, for about 20 seconds, until the butter melts and thickens the sauce.

Pour the sauce over the pork and serve immediately.

WAFU PASTA

In a country that loves its soba and udon, it shouldn't be surprising that Japanese have also embraced Italian-style pasta. But the pasta there is served in a uniquely *wafu* style—that is, tailored to local tastes using traditional ingredients, or created in a singularly Japanese way (see the story for "Napolitan" that follows, and you'll see what we mean).

Pasta was introduced to Japan by Westerners arriving in the late nineteenth century, who packed their staple noodles with them. A French missionary soon built the country's first macaroni factory in Nagasaki. But for years afterward, Italian pasta remained a rare and expensive food. Eventually, though, Japanese began producing these noodles themselves, and adapting them to their cuisine. Then the Americans arrived, after World War II, and brought with them mountains and mountains of spaghetti. In short order, schools started serving pasta, *wafu* pasta restaurants sprung up, and Italian noodles became a popular dish in homes across Japan—a popularity that shows no sign of abating.

We use spaghetti for the dishes in this section, but feel free to substitute with other kinds of pasta. Also, any of our *wafu* pasta dishes make great side dishes, not just the main meal.

"NAPOLITAN" SPAGHETTI

When the Americans arrived in Japan after World War II, they set up headquarters in the New Grand Hotel in Yokohama. A crowd of hungry GIs had to be fed, so the Americans arrived with truckloads of spaghetti at the ready, which they dished out liberally. The Japanese cooks at the hotel took notice. When the GIs eventually departed, they left behind cases of spaghetti and ketchup in the hotel stockrooms. What to do? An inventive hotel chef created a dish with spaghetti, sausage, and ketchup (tomatoes were too expensive at the time), and dubbed it "Napolitan." The people of Naples might not recognize this dish as their own, but, inexpensive and filling, it soon became a standard of school lunch menus across Japan. And what you eat as a kid, of course, is what you crave as an adult, and thus Napolitan happily entered the cuisine. If you'd like, you can substitute ham, bacon, or chicken for the sausage.

SERVES 4

1 pound dried spaghetti

2 tablespoons butter

4 ounces onion, sliced

4 ounces green pepper, cored and sliced

4 ounces white button mushrooms, trimmed

4 smoked sausages (about 8 ounces), sliced on an angle

1 teaspoon paprika

¼ cup sake

¼ cup milk

5 tablespoons ketchup

¼ cup grated Parmesan cheese

Tabasco sauce (optional)

Cook the pasta in a large pot of salted, boiling water (add 1 teaspoon of salt per pint of water). Follow package instructions for cooking, but remove the pasta from the water 1 minute earlier than specified, so the pasta is al dente.

While the pasta is cooking, melt the butter in a saucepan over medium heat. Add the onion, green pepper, and mushrooms, and cook, stirring constantly, for about 2 minutes. Add the sausage and cook for 2 minutes more, stirring frequently, to brown the sausage. Reduce the heat to low and add the paprika, sake, milk, and ketchup. Cook for about 5 minutes, mixing occasionally.

When the spaghetti is ready, drain in a colander. Add to the saucepan and toss for 30 seconds, so the pasta absorbs the flavors of the sauce. Turn off the heat and divide the pasta and sauce among 4 plates. Top with the Parmesan cheese and season with the Tabasco, to taste, and serve.

Yoshoku

MENTAIKO SPAGHETTI

This *wafu* pasta dish was invented by a Tokyo restaurant called Kabemo-ana in the 1960s, and its popularity quickly spread. Mentaiko is pollock roe marinated in chilies and salt, which turns the tiny eggs briny, buttery, and hot 'n' spicy—bold flavors that marry beautifully with pasta. The roe looks like a small red-colored sausage and can be found at Japanese markets. Cut open the sac to scoop out the roe. Do not cook mentaiko, which will kill its flavor. For garnish, you can also use 1/4 cup thinly sliced shiso leaves, 2 tablespoons chopped mitsuba, or 2 tablespoons sliced scallion.

SERVES 4

1 pound dried spaghetti

1/2 cup mentaiko (about 4 ounces), peeled and crumbled

4 teaspoons butter, softened

2 teaspoons soy sauce

2 teaspoons olive oil

2 teaspoons freshly squeezed lemon juice

2 tablespoons needle-cut nori or coarsely shredded nori sheets

Cook the pasta in a large pot of salted, boiling water (add 1 teaspoon of salt per pint of water). Follow package instructions for cooking, but remove the pasta from the water 1 minute earlier than specified, so pasta is al dente.

While the pasta is cooking, mix together the mentaiko, butter, soy sauce, olive oil, and lemon juice in a large bowl.

When the spaghetti is ready, strain in a colander, then add the pasta to the mentaiko mixture. Toss well, and divide among 4 plates. Garnish with the nori, and serve.

PASTA WITH MISO MEAT SAUCE

Like "Napolitan" (page 225) this pasta sounds Italian (meat sauce, then must be Bolognese), but it's anything but. In fact, its provenance is closer to Chinese *jajamen* noodles. With miso, spicy *toban-jan*, aromatics like toasted sesame oil and scallions, ginger and garlic, this pasta is packed with flavor and fragrance, and takes just minutes to prepare. If you can't find *Hatcho* miso, use only red miso for the recipe.

SERVES 4

1 cup torigara stock (page 25)

½ cup sake

1 teaspoon tobanjan (see page 236)

3 tablespoons mirin

2 tablespoons red miso (see page 234)

2 tablespoons Hatcho miso, or red miso like Sendai (see page 234)

1 teaspoon Japanese rice vinegar

1 pound dried spaghetti

2 tablespoons toasted sesame oil

1 tablespoon finely chopped ginger

1 tablespoon finely chopped garlic

2 tablespoons finely chopped scallion, white parts only

1 pound ground beef

4 teaspoons thinly sliced scallion

To make the sauce, add the *torigara*, sake, *tobanjan*, mirin, red miso, *Hatcho* miso, and vinegar to the work bowl of a blender. Pulse for about 1 minute, until smooth. Set aside.

Cook the pasta in a large pot of salted, boiling water (add 1 teaspoon of salt per pint of water). Follow package instructions for cooking, but remove the pasta from the water 1 minute earlier than specified, so pasta is al dente.

While the pasta is cooking, heat the sesame oil in a saucepan over medium heat. Add the ginger, garlic, and chopped scallion and cook, stirring constantly, for about 30 seconds. Add the ground beef and cook for about 1 minute, breaking apart the beef with chopsticks or a spoon as you cook. Add the reserved sauce. Reduce the heat to simmer and cook for about 5 minutes.

When the spaghetti is ready, drain in a colander. Add to the saucepan and toss for 30 seconds, so the pasta absorbs the flavors of the sauce. Turn off the heat and divide the pasta and sauce among 4 plates. Garnish with the sliced scallion and serve.

UNI PASTA

Uni—sea urchin—thrives in the cold, clear Sea of Japan waters off the coast of Hokkaido, in the country's far north. Harvested wild, it's enjoyed in Japan in a bunch of ways, as sashimi and sushi, in donburi (page 152), and also with pasta. In New York, we get amazing uni from California and Maine. If your fish shop or local Asian market carries it, try this dish. Use a good-quality extra-virgin olive oil to finish the pasta. If you want to make this dish richer, substitute 1 tablespoon butter for the ¼ cup olive oil, and add ¼ cup heavy cream with the water (reduce the water to ¾ cup).

¼ cup olive oil

¼ cup finely chopped onion

2 teaspoons finely chopped garlic

4 ounces shiitake mushrooms, stemmed and sliced

¼ cup sake

1 cup water

2 tablespoons soy sauce

4 ounces uni

1 teaspoon freshly squeezed lemon juice

1 pound dried spaghetti

4 teaspoons thinly sliced scallion, white and green parts

4 teaspoons extra-virgin olive oil

½ teaspoon salt

Pinch ground black pepper

Heat the ¼ cup olive oil in a saucepan over medium heat. Add the onion and garlic, and cook, stirring constantly, for about 30 seconds. Add the mushrooms and cook, stirring constantly, for 1 minute. Add the sake, and simmer for 30 seconds. Add the water and soy sauce. Cook for 30 seconds more and add the uni. Cook for 30 seconds, breaking apart the uni with chopsticks or a large spoon as it cooks. Turn off the heat and add the lemon juice.

Cook the pasta in a large pot of salted, boiling water (add 1 teaspoon of salt per pint of water). Follow package instructions for cooking, but remove the pasta from the water 1 minute earlier than specified, so pasta is al dente.

About 2 minutes before the pasta is ready, return the saucepan to low heat.

When the pasta is ready, strain in a colander. Add the pasta to the saucepan with the sauce. Add the scallion, olive oil, salt, and pepper. Toss the pasta with the ingredients for 30 seconds. Remove from the heat, and serve immediately.

Yoshoku

SHISO PASTA

This is an incredibly simple dish, perfect for summer cooking. You can find fresh shiso at Japanese markets (sometimes also called *ohba*). Like so many dishes in this book that are now Japanese household standards, this pasta was originally concocted at a restaurant, in this case a half century ago at Chianti, the first Italian dining establishment in Tokyo. The chefs there couldn't find basil, so they substituted that herb with an indigenous one, aromatic shiso, and fell in love with the results. Like basil, you can easily grow shiso in your garden or flowerpot and keep picking the leaves all summer long (find seeds online).

SERVES 4

1 pound dried spaghetti

20 shiso leaves, coarsely chopped

¼ cup olive oil

¼ cup ponzu (page 105)

2 teaspoons soy sauce

½ teaspoon freshly ground black pepper

½ teaspoon salt

Cook the pasta in plenty of salted, boiling water (add 1 teaspoon of salt per pint of water). Follow package instructions for cooking, but remove the pasta from the water 1 minute earlier than specified, so pasta is al dente.

While the pasta is cooking, mix together the shiso leaves, olive oil, ponzu, soy sauce, pepper, and salt in a large bowl.

When the spaghetti is ready, strain in a colander, then add the pasta to the shiso mixture. Toss well, and serve.

MUSHROOM WAFU PASTA

This is classic *wafu* cooking, using Japanese ingredients without butter or oil. We call for a trio of earthy, delicious cultivated Japanese mushrooms, but you can substitute with other mushrooms if you'd like (except for portobellos). When you cook this dish, it might look like too many mushrooms at first, but don't worry, the mushrooms cook down and the pasta will come out perfect!

SERVES 4

1 pound dried spaghetti

2 cups dashi (page 161)

¼ cup soy sauce

¼ cup mirin

8 ounces shiitake mushrooms, stemmed and sliced

1 package (about 3.5 ounces) shimeji mushrooms, trimmed and cut into bite-size pieces

1 package (about 7 ounces) enoki mushrooms, trimmed and cut into bite-size pieces

2 tablespoons katakuriko (potato starch) mixed with 2 tablespoons water

2 tablespoons thinly sliced scallion

1 teaspoon shichimi togarashi (see page 235)

Cook the pasta in a large pot of salted, boiling water (add 1 teaspoon of salt per pint of water). Follow package instructions for cooking, but remove the pasta from the water 1 minute earlier than specified, so pasta is al dente.

While the pasta is cooking, add the dashi, soy sauce, mirin, shiitake, shimeji, and enoki to a saucepan and bring to a boil over medium heat. Reduce the heat and simmer for about 3 minutes, until the mushrooms cook through. While the sauce is simmering, skim off any scum that appears on the surface.

Add the *katakuriko* mixture to the sauce, and cook for 30 seconds more, stirring to thicken the sauce. Turn off the heat.

When the spaghetti is ready, strain in a colander and divide among 4 plates. Pour the sauce and mushrooms over the pasta. Garnish with the scallion and *shichimi togarashi* and serve.

Yoshoku

ASARI PASTA

This is the Japanese version of pasta with clams. (*Asari* is the Japanese term for Manila clams.) The *yuzu kosho*, a citrusy, fiery condiment, adds heat and a heavenly aromatic touch. If you can, prepare the clam sauce while the pasta is cooking, so you can serve them together as soon as they're both ready, which tastes the best.

SERVES 4

1 pound dried spaghetti

¼ cup olive oil

2 tablespoons finely chopped onion

2 teaspoons finely chopped garlic

24 manila or small littleneck clams, scrubbed

1 cup sake

2 teaspoons red yuzu kosho (see page 236)

2 tablespoons butter

2 teaspoons soy sauce

2 tablespoons coarsely chopped mitsuba leaves

Cook the pasta in a large pot of salted, boiling water (add 1 teaspoon of salt per pint of water). Follow package instructions for cooking, but remove the pasta from the water 1 minute earlier than specified, so pasta is al dente. Strain the pasta in a colander and set aside.

While the pasta is cooking, heat the olive oil in a saucepan over medium heat. Add the onion and garlic, and cook, stirring constantly, for about 30 seconds. Add the clams, sake, and *yuzu kosho* and cover the saucepan. Cook until the clams open,

about 3 to 5 minutes. Discard any clams that don't open. Add the butter and soy sauce and simmer until the butter is melted, about 30 seconds. Turn off the heat.

When the spaghetti is ready, strain in a colander. Return the saucepan to medium heat. Add the pasta and toss for 30 seconds so the pasta absorbs the clam liquid. Divide the pasta, sauce, and clams among 4 plates. Garnish with the mitsuba and serve.

Yoshoku

JAPANESE INGREDIENTS

We wanted to explain in more detail some of the Japanese ingredients we use in the book. Please see the list below. Besides Japanese markets, you can often find these ingredients in Korean or Asian markets or online.

Japanese-Style Worcestershire Sauce, Tonkatsu Sauce, Okonomiyaki Sauce, Yakisoba Sauce

Japanese-style Worcestershire sauce is a derivation of the original British version. But instead of using fermented anchovies, as in the original, the Japanese sauce is based on purees of fruits and vegetables. Tonkatsu sauce is a thicker and sweeter style of this sauce, for tonkatsu (see Bulldog sauce, page 63). Okonomiyaki and yakisoba sauces are also adaptations of Japanese Worcestershire sauce made especially for their respective dishes. But you can also just use tonkatsu sauce (Bulldog) for okonomiyaki and yakisoba, as well as tonkatsu.

Karashi Mustard

Ground from a blend of pure mustard seed, *karashi* isn't cut with vinegar or other additives, so it's sinus-clearing potent. Use gingerly. It's sold as a paste in a tube or in powder form (mix with hot water to work into a thick paste). In Japanese markets *karashi* is also called "Japanese mustard," or "hot mustard."

Katakuriko

Katakuriko originally meant the starch from the *katakuri* plant. This kind of starch still exists but is rare and expensive, and not what we mean. Instead, what we're talking about is the *katakuriko* you find in Japanese markets, which is pure potato starch, despite its name. It usually comes in a clear plastic package that looks like a giant white sausage. If you can't find *katakuriko*, substitute cornstarch.

Kewpie

Japanese-style mayonnaise. See page 132.

Mirin

Mirin is a sweet cooking liquid more nuanced than sugar, and brewed from glutinous rice. It adds depth and umami-rich flavor as well as a shiny glaze to foods. Sometimes confusingly called "sweet sake," mirin is not sake but does contain alcohol.

Miso

Miso is a paste fermented from soybeans and salt, or soybeans, salt, and rice or barley. Hundreds of varieties of this classic Japanese staple are found across the country, but in this book we use two kinds.

Sendai miso is a salty, rice-based "red" miso that's aged to create a deep savory dimension and russet color. This miso hails from its namesake city of Sendai, has amazing flavor, and is ground to a coarse paste, which gives it a rustic feeling. If you can't find *Sendai* miso, use *shinshu aka* (*shinshu* red) or any other salty, rice-based red variety you can find (red miso is called *aka miso* in Japanese).

Hatcho miso is a dense, intense, chocolate-hued soybean-and-salt miso with an incredibly meaty savoriness. It's traditionally fermented in huge cedar barrels for at least two years. You can also substitute with aka dashi, which is *Hatcho* cut with white (*shiro*) miso and sometimes easier to find. (Or just use *Sendai* or *aka* miso.)

Mitsuba

Mistuba is clean, refreshing herb that resembles flat-leaf parsley. It has its own pleasing, distinctive flavor and is used as an accent on dishes.

Negi

Negi is a Japanese onion with long white cylinders that grow up to 2 feet long and 3/4 inch thick and that sprouts green leaves at the top (technically called *Tokyo negi* or *naga negi*, as there are many varieties in Japan). Unless we indicate otherwise, use the entire onion, including the green parts, but trim off any dry leaves. Please note that this onion is also sometimes confusingly called "Japanese leek" (although not a leek) or "welsh onion" (no connection to Wales). If you can't find them, substitute with two large scallions per negi in the recipes.

Nira

Nira are Japanese garlic chives; they're deep green and look like large grass leaves.

Rayu

Rayu is Japanese-style chili oil that's made from sesame oil infused with chili peppers. It's available in bottles at Asian markets, or you can make it yourself (see our recipe, page 35).

Sake

Sake is the quintessential Japanese alcoholic drink, but it's also a fundamental cooking ingredient. Brewed from rice through a process that's closer to brewing beer than making wine (so calling it "rice wine" is a misnomer), sake adds umami, sweetness, acidity, and depth to foods.

Shichimi Togarashi and *Ichimi Togarashi*

Shichimi togarashi is a popular Japanese spice originated in the 1600s and is made from a mixture of seven ingredients, including ground chili, *sansho*, sesame seed, and other aromatics. *Ichimi togarashi* is just pure ground chili.

Shiso

A member of the mint family, this plant has tender, fragrant heart-shaped leaves with distinctive sawtooth edges. There are two kinds of shiso, purple and green. The green variety (also called *ohba*) is commonly available here. Discard the stems and use only the leaves in dishes.

Shoyu (Soy Sauce)

Fermented from soybeans and wheat, soy sauce adds character, umami-driven savoriness, and caramel flavor and color to foods. There are two main styles: *koikuchi* is the all-purpose, standard Japanese soy sauce that's readily available at Asian and Japanese markets (like the brand Kikkoman, which you can also find in supermarkets). *Usukuchi* is a lighter-colored but saltier soy sauce that hails from the Kansai region (around Kyoto). Unless we specify otherwise, use the all-purpose *koikuchi* for our recipes.

Tobanjan

This spicy red paste is fermented from fava beans and chilies, and was originally a Chinese culinary import to Japan.

Wasabi

The fragrance, clean flavor, and subtle heat of this classic Japanese ingredient enliven the palate like nothing else. A rhizome with lime-colored flesh, fresh wasabi is expensive and hard to get here. If you can find it, grate with a fine grater. Alternatives are pure wasabi paste in a tube or an economical wasabi-flavored mixture sold in a tube or as a powder (mix with water to work into a thick paste).

Yuzu Kosho

One of our favorite Japanese condiments, *yuzu kosho* is an alluring, aromatic marriage of fiery chilies, salt, and tangy Japanese *yuzu* citrus zest and juice. This cured paste comes in two styles: red, with a more rounded flavor, and the sharper green. Both add palate-popping flavor and heat.

TOKYO COMFORT FOOD RESTAURANTS

Tokyo is home to thousands of restaurants. The following are a few of our favorite real-deal joints that cook up the dishes we share in the book. They're all Japanese speaking only, but don't let that discourage you.

Asakusa Okonomiyaki Sometaro

2-2-2, Nishiasakusa, Taito-ku, Tokyo 111-0035
03-3844-9502
www.sometaro.com

Set in a traditional Japanese structure, this is an old-school Tokyo restaurant, one that specializes in okonomiyaki.

Kameido Gyoza

5-3-3, Kameido, Koto-ku, Tokyo 136-0071
03-3681-8854

This tiny neighborhood shop specializes in just one dish—gyoza. Gyoza and a frosty beer, what else do you need?

Kanda Matsuya

1-13, Sudacho, Kanda, Chiyoda-ku,
Tokyo 101-0041
03-3251-1556
kanda-matsuya.jp

Founded in 1884, this traditional soba joint rolls noodles by hand in front of the customers and serves unbelievably good tempura soba.

Pasta Kabenoana

1F, Kasumi Bldg., 2-25-17, Dogenzaka,
Shibuya-ku, Tokyo 150-0043
03-3770-8305
www.kabenoana.com/index.html

Since its opening in 1953, this restaurant has created innovative wafu pasta dishes, including mentaiko spaghetti (page 226), which is now popular across Japan.

Ramen Tenjinshita Daiki

1F, Shiraki Bldg., 3-47-2, Yushima, Bunkyo-ku,
Tokyo 113-0034
03-3834-0348
www.daiki1999.com/eng/index.html

Chef Kazuyuki Takekawa creates some of the finest Tokyo-style shoyu ramen in Japan at this shop, preparing everything by hand, from the stock to the noodles. Amazing ramen.

Rengatei

3-5-16, Ginza, Chuo-ku, Tokyo 104-0061
03-3561-3882
www.ginza-rengatei.com/index1f.html

Founded in 1895 and still going strong today, this is the restaurant where tonkatsu (page 60), kaki furai (page 78), omu rice (page 215), and other comfort food standards were first created.

Shōryū

6-10-14, Ueno, Taito-ku, Tokyo 103-0011
03-3832-0827

Nestled in an alley off the busy Ameyo Kocho market, the piece de resistance of this tiny joint is their giant, amazing 6-inch-long gyoza.

Tamahide

1-17-10, Ningyōchō, Nihonbashi, Chuo-ku, Tokyo 103-0013
03-3668-7651
www.tamahide.co.jp

Opened in 1760, this classic restaurant is the birthplace of oyakodon and other dishes. Also check out Ningyōchō's traditional market street nearby.

Yoshikami

1-41-4 Asakusa, Taito-ku, Tokyo 111-0032
03-3841-1802
www.yoshikami.co.jp

Founded in 1951 and now an institution, Yoshikami specializes in yoshoku cooking (page 206). Tadashi first came here with his dad as a boy and has been returning ever since.

MEASUREMENT CONVERSION CHARTS

Volume

U.S.	Imperial	Metric
1 tablespoon	1/2 fl oz	15 ml
2 tablespoons	1 fl oz	30 ml
1/4 cup	2 fl oz	60 ml
1/3 cup	3 fl oz	90 ml
1/2 cup	4 fl oz	120 ml
2/3 cup	5 fl oz (1/4 pint)	150 ml
3/4 cup	6 fl oz	180 ml
1 cup	8 fl oz (1/3 pint)	240 ml
1 1/4 cups	10 fl oz (1/2 pint)	300 ml
2 cups (1 pint)	16 fl oz (2/3 pint)	480 ml
2 1/2 cups	20 fl oz (1 pint)	600 ml
1 quart	32 fl oz (1 2/3 pints)	1 l

Temperature

Fahrenheit	Celsius/Gas Mark
250°F	120°C/gas mark 1/2
275°F	135°C/gas mark 1
300°F	150°C/gas mark 2
325°F	160°C/gas mark 3
350°F	180 or 175°C/gas mark 4
375°F	190°C/gas mark 5
400°F	200°C/gas mark 6
425°F	220°C/gas mark 7
450°F	230°C/gas mark 8
475°F	245°C/gas mark 9
500°F	260°C

Length

Inch	Metric
1/4 inch	6 mm
1/2 inch	1.25 cm
3/4 inch	2 cm
1 inch	2.5 cm
6 inches (1/2 foot)	15 cm
12 inches (1 foot)	30 cm

Weight

U.S./Imperial	Metric
1/2 oz	15 g
1 oz	30 g
2 oz	60 g
1/4 lb	115 g
1/3 lb	150 g
1/2 lb	225 g
3/4 lb	350 g
1 lb	450 g

ABOUT THE AUTHORS

Tadashi Ono is a Japanese chef and author based in New York City. He has been featured in the *New York Times, Gourmet,* and *Food & Wine.*

Harris Salat's stories about food and culture have appeared in the *New York Times, Saveur,* and *Gourmet*. In 2012, Salat opened the Japanese comfort food restaurant Ganso in Brooklyn (gansonyc.com). He is the author, with Takashi Yagihashi, of *Takashi's Noodles.*

Together, Ono and Salat are the authors of *Japanese Hot Pots* and *The Japanese Grill.*

INDEX

Copyright © 2013 by Tadashi Ono and Harris Salat
Photographs copyright © 2013 by Todd Coleman

Published in the United States by Ten Speed Press,
an imprint of the Crown Publishing Group,
a division of Random House, Inc., New York.
www.crownpublishing.com
www.tenspeed.com

Ten Speed Press and the Ten Speed Press colophon are
registered trademarks of Random House, Inc.

Library of Congress Cataloging-in-Publication Data
Ono, Tadashi, 1962- author.
Japanese soul cooking : ramen, tonkatsu, tempura, and
more from the streets and kitchens of tokyo and beyond /
Tadashi Ono and Harris Salat.
    pages cm
Includes index.
1. Cooking, Japanese. I. Salat, Harris, author. II. Title.
TX724.5.J3O564 2013
641.5952--dc23

                    2013020776

Hardcover ISBN: 978-1-60774-352-1
eBook ISBN: 978-1-60774-353-8

Printed in China

Design by Toni Tajima

10 9 8 7 6 5 4 3 2 1

First Edition